ON THE NAME

MERIDIAN

Crossing Aesthetics

Werner Hamacher

& David E. Wellbery

Editors

Edited by
Thomas Dutoit

Stanford
University
Press

Stanford
California
1995

ON THE NAME

Jacques Derrida

Originally published in French in 1993
as three separate booklets: *Passions*,
Sauf le nom, and *Khōra* by Editions Galilée.
© 1993 by Editions Galilée

Stanford University Press
Stanford, California
© 1995 by the Board of Trustees
of the Leland Stanford Junior University

Printed in the United States of America

CIP data appear at the end of the book

Stanford University Press publications
are distributed exclusively by
Stanford University Press within the
United States, Canada, Mexico, and Central America;
they are distributed exclusively by
Cambridge University Press throughout
the rest of the world.

Contents

Translating the Name?

Jacques Derrida's *On the Name* comprises three essays, which, if taken together, would "form a sort of *Essay on the Name*" (see below p. xiv). In 1993 the three essays simultaneously appeared in France as a *Collection* of three separately bound but matching books published by Editions Galilée. *On the Name*, the title of this book published by Stanford University Press, thus is not a translation of any French book title by Jacques Derrida; it is a name given to what is a hypothetical book in France. The title *On the Name* would in French be *Sur le nom*. Given the meanings of the French preposition *sur*, one could call this book by other names as well: for example, *Over the Name*, *Above the Name*, or *About the Name*. (One should also be aware in this title of the "no" [*non*] which in spoken French sounds exactly the same as "name" [*nom*], especially in view of what the first essay says about homonymy and the second essay's concern with a certain negativity.) Moreover, given Derrida's discussion of "sur-naming," which runs through the three essays, one might justifiably also read *sur le nom* (on the name) in the inverted order of *le surnom* (the sur-name), with *sur* as the prefix that it is in English and French.

The translation throughout this volume of *surnom* by "sur-name" could cause some confusion. *Surnom* means a name, title, or epithet added to a person's name, as in a "nickname" such as Earvin "Magic" Johnson or William "the Conqueror." The English "sur-name" is thus roughly synonymous with "cognomen" or "to-name," as the *OED* attests. Moreover, just as *surnom* gives us the sense of "surname" in William "the Conqueror," the Norman Conquest is said to have given us the other meaning of "surname," which *surnom* no longer has: "The Norman Conquest . . . brought with it the novelty of family nomenclature, that is to say, the use of hereditary surnames" (Edward A. Freeman, *History of the Norman Conquest of England* [New York: Macmillan, 1876], 5: 377). In English the word "surname" still means (and this has even become its primary meaning) the "family name" that follows one's first, given, or baptismal name, i.e., that follows one's "pre-name" or *prénom* as it is called in French. Unlike the English language, the French language, in its modern usage, has not retained this meaning of *surnom*. Indeed, the expression "connaître quelqu'un par nom et par surnom," an expression which means "to know someone very well," clearly shows that in French the *nom* (family name) is something different from the *surnom* (sur-name as nickname).

As the "surname" as "nickname" can supplement a given name to the point of replacing it—as Freeman puts it, "in some cases the surname or nickname seems to have altogether supplanted the baptismal name" (377)—so too has "surname" in the contemporary English sense of a hereditary "family name" supplanted "surname" in the French sense of *surnom* or "nickname." Because of this difference between *surnom* and "surname" in contemporary French and English, *surnom* is translated in these three essays as "sur-name," with the hyphen serving to call attention to the "sur-name" as the "supplemental name" that any surname in fact is. It is necessary to keep "sur-name" instead of "nickname" as noun and verb for *surnom* and *surnommer* because in Derrida's French text their function is too important not to be carried over into English, even though in English they bear a sense not admitted in modern French.

The potential confusion between "surname" as added name and "surname" as family name is perhaps owing to the fact that the family name is originally, as Freeman contends, only a "surname" in the sense of an added name that at some point became hereditary. In this way, the "family name" is itself always just a hereditary nickname, as "the surname of Black may be borne by a pale man, that of Alfredson by one whose father is not named Alfred, that of Fecham by one who neither lives at Fecham nor owns land there" (378). If one's "family name," the proper name, is originally lacking in such a way that a nickname, a sur-name, must, by *repetition*, fill its lack, then one's name, one's fame, one's renown comes before anything else through an act of *re-naming*. Perhaps such is part of what Derrida suggests when he asks: "What happens, above all, when it is necessary to sur-name [*surnommer*], re-naming there where, precisely, the name comes to be found lacking?" (below, p. xiv). The sur-name, by repetition or "re-naming," constitutes the proper name.

Moreover, the translation of *re-nommant* by "re-naming" fails to retain the complexity of *re-nommant*. To begin with, *renommer* and its deceptive cognate "to rename" are not normally hyphenated. In other contexts, without the hyphen, *renommant* might commonly be translated as "reappointing" or "re-electing." *Renommer* also means "to name often and with praise, to celebrate." If someone has, in everyday French, *renom*, she or he has "name-recognition," celebrity, or popularity in mainly a positive sense. *Renom* thus gives "renown." (One should recall the word "name" in both "nown" or "noun" and *renom*; French has only *nom* for both "noun" and "name.") Also, the noun *renommée* is "renown" or "fame." This semantic field is active in Derrida's essays. Yet in the quote above, the hyphen in *re-nommant* stresses the repetition of naming, of naming as originally re-naming, a repetition that in the sur-name first constitutes the name, the proper name. The surname is a repetition (and a forgetting) that conceals the sur-name, itself a repetition.

This superimposition of one surname ("family name") onto another (the sur-name) is part of what the *surnom* or "sur-name" says by definition, for the prefix "sur," derived from Latin *super*, allows one to read, as Derrida at times does, *surnommer* or sur-naming as "supernaming," "overnaming," "extra" or "excess" naming. Conveying while distinguishing these various senses of "sur-naming" and of "re-naming" is part of the task of translating and reading the three essays that make up *On the Name*.

Two of the titles given to these three essays require brief comment. In the third, *Khōra*, Derrida has, in keeping with recent French practice, preferred to transcribe the Greek letter χ (*khi*) with "kh" instead of "ch" (thus *khōra* for χώρα, instead of *chōra*, as it has customarily been transcribed). Moreover, *khōra* is a feminine noun, and in Derrida's text the pronoun that replaces it is the feminine *elle* or "she." Indeed, rather than writing "the *khōra*" as commentators have always done, Derrida writes simply "*khōra*," as if "*khōra*" were a feminine given name. In the beginning of the English text, Geoffrey Bennington translates *elle* by "it," for there the sense of *elle* is that of an impersonal "it." Yet as the essay progresses, this *elle* gradually becomes appropriately translated by "she."

Both readers familiar with Plato's *Timaeus* and those coming to it first through Derrida's *Khōra* will see that *Khōra* designates a very problematic space, place, or site. Bennington's translation of terms such as *lieu, place,* and *site* has carefully distinguished these terms and the various idioms in which they occur. Where Derrida distinguishes *places* and *lieu(x)* in conjunction, the translation chooses "places" and "site(s)"; English "positions" should also be heard in the French *places*. Another instance of *place* being translated by "place" is the translation of the expression *prendre place* by "to take place," where the sense is more a "place" or a "position" being "taken" than "to happen." "Site(s)" is used for *lieu(x)* only where *lieu* and *place* are in proximity; otherwise "site" translates *site*, and "place" translates *lieu*. The particular distinction between "places" (*places*) and "site(s)" (*lieu[x]*) should not obscure another distinction operating in *Khōra*, that between "to situate" (*situer*) and "to give place" (*donner lieu*).

There is really no one adequate English translation for *Sauf le nom*. The most apparent sense in English would be "Except the name." *Sauf le nom* means precisely that; thus, for example, when Derrida writes *tout sauf le nom*, the sense is "everything except the name." But the preposition "except" fails to convey the other sense

of *sauf*, which as an adjective means "safe." A less obvious translation of *sauf le nom* is "safe the name," which should be read with an
intonation that pauses after "safe." Transcribed, that intonation
would be "safe, the name." In better, more grammatical English,
the sense is that "the name is safe," even the subjunctive "that the
name be safe"; thus, for example, *tout sauf le nom* then would be in
English "totally safe the name," which may be understood in the
indicative as "the name is totally safe" or in the subjunctive as "that
the name be totally safe." "Except" for *sauf* is unfortunate because
it loses the signified "safe." There would seem to be an alternative:
the somewhat literary "save" is synonymous with "except." Thus,
sauf le nom would be "save the name," which could be understood
exactly as "except the name." The danger with "save," however, is
that it sounds like a verb in the imperative mood. In the French
sauf le nom, there is no imperative whatsoever. "Sauf" is not a verb,
but either a preposition—more common than its English cognate
"save"—or an adjective. "Save the Name" would be an unfortunate
English title for *Sauf le nom*, since it would sound as if the essay
were a call to "save the name," a sense that appears in the text only
discreetly. Even though "Save the Name" as a title might be better
than "Except the Name" or "Safe, the Name," such a title would
risk giving a false sense of what the essay is about.

Therefore, owing to the double syntax of *sauf le nom*, everything
in the essay has been translated "save its name," or title. Yet within
the essay itself "save the name" has been used to translate the
prepositional phrase *sauf le nom*, and "safe, the name" has been
added after it in brackets where the possibility of understanding
that adjectival phrase is also present.

Of the three essays in *On the Name*, *Passions*, translated by David
Wood, appeared originally in English and in a shorter form in
Derrida: A Critical Reader, edited by David Wood (Oxford: Basil
Blackwell, 1992). An earlier, shorter version of *Sauf le nom* appeared
for the first time also in English, in the translation of John P.
Leavey, Jr., under the title "Post-Scriptum" in a volume entitled
Derrida and Negative Theology, edited by Harold Coward and Toby
Foshay (Albany: State University of New York Press, 1992). They

appear here courtesy of these publishers. *Khōra*, translated by
Geoffrey Bennington, appears here for the first time in English, in
a revised version from how it originally appeared, in French, in
Poikilia: Etudes offertes à Jean-Pierre Vernant (Paris: Ecole des
Hautes Etudes en Sciences Sociales, 1987). In *On the Name*, these
three translations have been occasionally modified so that common
elements harmonize and so that each corresponds to the more
recent versions of *Passions, Sauf le nom*, and *Khōra* published by
Editions Galilée.

When the three books were published in France, each included
an unbound, four-page insert, called in French the *Prière d'insérer*
and serving there, as well as here, to articulate the three:

> Each of these three essays, *Passions, Sauf le nom*, and *Khōra*, forms an
> independent work and can be read as such. If it has nonetheless been
> judged advisable to publish them simultaneously, this is because, in
> spite of the singular origin of each of them, the same thematic thread
> runs through the three. They form a sort of *Essay on the Name*—in
> three chapters or three steps. Three fictions, too. In following the signs
> that the *dramatis personae* of these fictions silently address one to the
> other, one can hear the *question of the name* resound there where it
> hesitates on the edge of the call, of the demand or of the promise,
> before or after the response.
>
> The name: What does one call thus? What does one understand
> under the name of name? And what occurs when one gives a name?
> What does one give then? One does not offer a thing, one delivers
> nothing, and still something comes to be which comes down to giving
> that which one does not have, as Plotinus said of the Good. What
> happens, above all, when it is necessary to sur-name [*surnommer*], re-
> naming there where, precisely, the name comes to be found lacking?
> What makes the proper name into a sort of sur-name, pseudonym, or
> cryptonym at once singular and singularly untranslatable?
>
> *Passions* says an absolute secret, at once essential and foreign to what
> one in general calls by the noun/name secret. In order to get there, it
> was necessary, within the more or less fictive repetition of a "this is my
> body," and in the course of a meditation on the paradoxes of polite-
> ness, to stage the experience of where an incalculable debt flares up: if
> there is duty [*du devoir*], shouldn't it consist in not having to [*ne pas*

devoir], in having to without having to [*devoir sans devoir*], in having
to not have to [*devoir ne pas devoir*]? In having to not have to act [*à
devoir ne pas devoir agir*] "in conformity with duty [*devoir*]," not even,
as Kant would say, "by duty [*devoir*]"? What could the ethical or
political consequences of that be? What should one understand under
the name "duty" [*devoir*]? And who can undertake to carry it, in and
through responsibility?

Sauf le nom. It's a matter here of salutation and salvation [*du salut*;
the familiar greeting *salut* is also to wish for the other's salvation or
happiness]. On a summer day, two interlocutors converse—that's
another fiction—about what turns around [*tourne autour*] the name,
singularly around the name of name, the name of God [*Dieu*] and
what becomes of it in what one calls negative theology, there where the
Sur-Name names the unnamable, that is, at the same time what one
neither *can* nor *should* name, define, or know, because, to begin with,
what one sur-names then slips away *beyond being*, without staying
there. Where "negative theology" seems to open onto a "politics" to
come (today or tomorrow), such a fiction also risks taking a few steps
of an heir who follows the traces or vestiges as a "cherubinic wanderer"
(Angelus Silesius). What is a Sur-Name, that which is worth *more than*
the name but also that which comes *in the place* of the name? And does
it ever put itself forward as the salvation [*salut*] of the name, which is
finally *Safe*? And very simply, as the salutation, very simply, the "Good
Day" or the "farewell" [*adieu*]?

Khōra, the oldest of the three essays, is nonetheless not their "matrix" or the originary "imprint-bearer," as one might be tempted to
consider it. It only situates an exemplary aporia in the Platonic text.
The *Timaeus* names *khōra* (locality, place, spacing, site), this "thing"
that is nothing of that to which this "thing" nonetheless seems to "give
place"—without, however, this "thing" ever *giving* anything: neither
the ideal paradigms of things nor the copies that an insistent demiurge, the fixed idea before his eyes, inscribes in it. Insensible, impassible but without cruelty, inaccessible to rhetoric, *Khōra* discourages, it
"is" precisely what disarms efforts at persuasion—and whoever would
like to find the heart to believe or the desire to make believe: for
example, in the figures, tropes, or seductions of discourse. Neither
sensible nor intelligible, neither metaphor nor literal designation,
neither this *nor* that, *both* this *and* that, participating and not participating in the two terms of a couple, *khōra*—also called "matrix" or

"nurse"—nonetheless resembles a singular proper name, a *pre*-name [pré*nom*, here literally, colloquially one's "first name"] that is earlier, both maternal and virginal (this is why one says here *khōra* and not, as usual, the *khōra*) even though, in an experience that has to be thought, it/she both calls in silence the sur-name that one gives to her and stands beyond every maternal, feminine—or theological—figure. And this silence, from the depths of which *khōra* thus seems to call her name but in truth calls the sur-name of a first name [*prénom*], this silence is perhaps not even any longer a modality or a reserve of speech. No more than this depth without depth promises the night of a day. On the subject of *khōra*, there is neither negative theology nor thought of the Good, of the One, or of God beyond Being. This incredible and improbable experience is also, among other dimensions, *political*. It announces, without promising, a thought, or rather, a putting to test of the political. And when Socrates makes a show of addressing himself to the others and of speaking of *politeia* in passing (and as the passerby he is, in a life that is too short), there he begins to resemble it, to resemble her, *khōra*, to play her in a fiction that will always have gone unnoticed, to figure her, her who is the intangible, the ungrasp-able, the improbable, totally near and infinitely far away, her who receives everything beyond exchange and beyond the gift. Her as what *is necessary* [il faut] still, *Necessity*, without debt.

In addition to this insert, each of the books included the follow-ing passage, following a statement of the essay's publication history:

In spite of all that separates them, these texts seem to respond to each other, and maybe to shed light on each other within a single configura-tion. Under the mobile syntax of these titles, one could read *three essays on a name given* or on what can *happen to the name given* (anonymity, metonymy, paleonymy, cryptonomy, pseudonymity), hence to the name *received*, indeed, to the name *owed* [*nom* dû], on what perhaps one *ought* to give or to sacrifice as well as what one *owes* [*ce que peut-être l'on* doit] to the name, to the name of name, hence to the sur-name, and to the name of the *duty* [devoir] (*to give or to receive*).

—*Thomas Dutoit*

PASSIONS

NOTE: A certain "context" forms the theme or center [*foyer*] of these reflections. Some contextual instructions are therefore especially necessary for reading a "response" whose original version (slightly modified here) was translated by David Wood and published in English in a work entitled *Derrida: A Critical Reader*, edited by David Wood (Oxford: Blackwell, 1992). The work contained twelve essays; the present essay, in principle, was supposed to respond to the others. In the Anglo-Saxon tradition of the "Reader," this collection of essays was nonetheless conceived of less as an introduction or commentary, and even less as homage, than as the place for a critical discussion, as its title indicated. The participants in this discussion were Geoffrey Bennington, Robert Bernasconi, Michel Haar, Irene Harvey, Manfred Frank, John Llewelyn, Jean-Luc Nancy, Christopher Norris, Richard Rorty, John Sallis, and David Wood.

§ Passions:
"An Oblique Offering"

Let us imagine a scholar. A specialist in ritual analysis, he seizes upon this work, assuming that someone has not presented him with it (something we will never know). At any rate, he makes quite a thing of it, believing he can recognize in it the ritualized unfolding of a ceremony, or even a liturgy, and this becomes a theme, an *object* of analysis for him. Ritual, to be sure, does not define a field. There is ritual everywhere. Without it, there would be no society, no institutions, no history. Anyone can specialize in the analysis of rituals; it is not therefore a specialty. This scholar, let us call him an analyst, may also be, for example, a sociologist, an anthropologist, a historian, whatever you prefer, an art critic or a literary critic, perhaps even a philosopher. You or me. Through experience and more or less spontaneously, each of us can to some degree play the part of an analyst or critic of rituals; no one refrains from it. Moreover, to play a role in this work, to *play a role* wherever it may be, one must at the same time be inscribed in the logic of ritual and, precisely so as to perform properly in it, to avoid mistakes and transgressions, one must to some extent be able to analyze it. One must understand its norms and interpret the rules of its functioning.

Between the actor and the analyst, whatever the distance or differences may be, the boundary therefore appears uncertain. Always permeable. It *must* even be crossed at some point not only

3

for there to be analysis at all but also for behavior to be appropriate and ritualized normally.

But a "critical reader" would quite properly object that not all analyses are equivalent. Is there not an essential difference between, on the one hand, the analysis of him or her who, in order to participate *properly* in a ritual, must understand its norms, and an analysis which, instead of aligning itself with the ritual, tries to explain it, to "objectify" it, to give an account of its principle and of its purpose? A critical difference, to be exact? Perhaps, but what is a critical difference? Because in the end if he is to analyze, read, or interpret, the participant must also maintain a certain critical position. And in a certain manner, an "objectifying" position. Even if his activity is often close to passivity, if not passion, the participant goes on to critical and criteriological acts: a vigilant discrimination is required from whoever, in one capacity or another, becomes an interested party in the ritual process (the agent, the beneficiary, the priest, the sacrificer, the property man, and even the excluded, the victim, the villain or the *pharmakos*, who may be the offering itself, because the offering is never a simple thing, but already a discourse, at least the possibility of a discourse, putting a symbolicity to work). The participant must make choices, distinguish, differentiate, evaluate. He must operate according to some *krinein*. Even the "spectator," here the reader, in the volume or outside the volume, finds himself in the same situation in this regard. Instead of opposing critique to noncritique, instead of choosing or deciding between critique and noncritique, objectivity and its contrary, it would be necessary, then, both to mark the differences between the critiques and to situate the noncritical in a place which would no longer be opposed to, nor even perhaps exterior to, critique. Critique and noncritique are surely not identical, but, deep down, they may remain the same. In any case, they participate in the same.

I

Let us then imagine this work being proposed (delivered, offered, given) to a reader-analyst concerned with objectivity. This analyst may be among us: any recipient or sender of this book. We can imagine that without making available an unlimited credit to such a reader. At any rate the analyst (I choose this word, of course, with the use that Poe made of it in mind)[1] would be sure, perhaps rashly, that he had come across the coded unfolding of a ceremony, an unfolding both foreseeable and prescribed. *Ceremony* is doubtless the most precise and the richest word to bring together all the aspects [*traits*] of the event. How could I, then, how could you, how could we, how could they, not be ceremonious? What precisely is the subject of a ceremony?

But it is here in the description and the analysis of ritual, in deciphering it or, if you prefer, in reading it, that a difficulty suddenly arises, a sort of dysfunctioning, what could be called a crisis. In short, a *critical* moment. Perhaps it would affect the very unfolding of the symbolic process.

What crisis? Was it foreseeable or unforeseeable? And what if the crisis even concerned the very concept of crisis or of critique?

Some philosophers have got together or have been gathered together by academic and editorial procedures familiar to *us*. Let us emphasize the critical determination (impossible because open, open to *you*, precisely) of this personal pronoun: who is "us," who are we precisely? These philosophers, university academics from different countries, are known and nearly all know each other (here would follow a detailed description of each of them, of their type and of their singularity, of their sexual allegiance—only one woman —of their national affiliation, of their socio-academic status, of their past, their publications, their interests, etc.). So, on the initiative of one of them, who cannot be just any one and is someone whose interests are certainly not uninteresting, they agreed to get together and participate in a volume whose focus (relatively determinate, thus indeterminate, one could say secret up to a certain point—and the crisis remains too open to merit the name of crisis yet) will be such and such (relatively determined, etc., relatively identifiable, in principle, by his work, his publications, his proper name, his signatures, "signatures" being perhaps best left in the plural, because it is impossible, at the outset, and even if legal, illegitimate, to preclude their multiplicity). If a critical

difficulty arises in this case, one likely—but this is not yet certain—
to put in difficulty the programmes of ritual or of its analysis, it
does not necessarily have to do with the content, the theses, the
positive or negative evaluations, most often infinitely overdetermined. It need not, in short, concern the quality of the discourse of
this or that person, what they translate, or what they make of their
relation to the title, to the pretext, or to the object of the book. The
critical difficulty concerns the fact that it has been thought necessary to ask, propose, or offer (for reasons which it is possible to
analyze) to the supposed signatory of the texts which are the focus
of the book ("me," surely?) the opportunity of intervening, as they
say, of "contributing," which means bringing one's tribute, but
doing so freely, *in the book*. We will have something to say in due
course about the extent of this freedom; it is almost the entire
question. The editor of the work, head of protocol or master of
ceremonies, David Wood, had suggested that the book might here
even begin with a few pages of text which, without truly responding to all the others, could appear under the suggestive title of "An
Oblique Offering." What? From whom? To whom? (More of this
later.)

But straightaway, as we were saying, the unfolding of the ritual
risks losing its automatic quality, that is to say, it risks no longer
conforming to the first hypothesis of the analyst. There is a second
hypothesis. Which? At a certain place in the system, one of the
elements of the system (an "I," surely, even if the I is not always,
and "with all . . . candor" [*sans façon*: also "without further ado"][2]
"me") no longer knows what it should do. More precisely it knows
that it must do contradictory and incompatible things. Contradict-
ing or running counter to itself, this double obligation thus risks
paralyzing, diverting, or jeopardizing the successful conclusion of
the ceremony. But does the hypothesis of such a risk *go against* [à
l'encontre] or on the contrary *go along with* [à la rencontre] the
desire of the participants, supposing that there were only one
desire, that there were a single desire common to all of them or that
each had in himself only one noncontradictory desire? Because one
can imagine that one or more than one participant, indeed the

master of ceremonies himself, may somehow desire the failure of the aforementioned ceremony. More or less secretly, it goes without saying, and that is why we must *tell* the secret, not reveal it, but with the example of this secret, pass judgment on the secret in general.

What is a secret?

Certainly, even if this work in no way corresponds to a secret ceremony, one may imagine that there is no ceremony, however public and exposed, which does not revolve around a secret, even if it is the secret of a nonsecret, if only what one calls in French a *secret de Polichinelle*, a secret which is a secret for no one. On the analyst's first hypothesis, the ceremony would unfold normally, according to the ritual; it would achieve its end at the cost of a detour or of a suspense which not only would not have at all threatened it, but would perhaps have confirmed, consolidated, augmented, embellished, or intensified it by an expectation (desire, premium of seduction, preliminary pleasure of play, foreplay [*prélude*], what Freud calls *Vorlust*). But what would happen on the second hypothesis? This is perhaps the question that, by way of a replay and as a token of boundless gratitude, I would like to ask, I, in my turn, and in the first instance to all those who have generously brought their tribute [*apporter leur tribut*] to this work.

Friendship as well as politeness would enjoin a double *duty*: would it not precisely be to avoid at all cost both the *language of ritual* and the *language of duty*? Duplicity, the being-double of this duty, cannot be added up as a 1 + 1 = 2 or a 1 + 2, but on the contrary hollows itself out in an infinite abyss. A gesture "of friendship" or "of politeness" would be neither friendly nor polite if it were purely and simply to obey a ritual rule. But this *duty* to eschew the rule of ritualized decorum also demands that one go beyond the very language of *duty*. One must not be friendly or polite out of duty. We venture such a proposition, without a doubt, against Kant. Would there thus be a duty not to act *according to duty*: neither *in conformity to duty*, as Kant would say (*pflichtmässig*), nor even *out of duty* (*aus Pflicht*)? In what way would such a duty, or such a counter-duty, indebt us? According to what? According to whom?

Taken seriously, this hypothesis in the form of a question would be enough to give one vertigo. It would make one tremble, it could also paralyze one at the edge of the abyss, there where you would be alone, all alone or already caught up in a struggle with the other, an other who would seek in vain to hold you back or to push you into the void, to save you or to lose you. Always supposing—we shall return to this—that one ever had any choice in this matter.

Because we already risk no longer knowing where the evidence could lead us, let us venture to state the double axiom involved in the hypothesis or in the question with which we inevitably had to begin. Doubtless it would be impolite to appear to be making a gesture, for example, in responding to an invitation, out of simple duty. It would also be unfriendly to respond to a friend out of duty. It would be no better to respond to an invitation or to a friend in conformity with duty, *pflichtmässig* (rather than out of duty, *aus Pflicht*, and we cite once more the *Groundwork for a Metaphysics of Morals* of Kant, our exemplary "critical reader" [in English in original—Ed.], indebted as we are, as his heirs, to the great philosopher of critique). That would indeed add to the essential dereliction, one further fault: to consider oneself beyond reproach by playing on appearances just where intention is in default. It is insufficient to say that the "ought" [*il faut*] of friendship, like that of politeness, *must not be on the order of duty*. It must not even take the form of a rule, and certainly not of a ritual rule. As soon as it yields to the necessity of applying the generality of a prescription to a single case, the gesture of friendship or of politeness would itself be destroyed. It would be defeated, beaten, and broken by the ordered rigidity of rules, or, put a different way, of norms. An axiom from which it is not necessary to conclude further that one can only accede to friendship or politeness (for example, in responding to an invitation, or indeed to the request or the question of a friend) by transgressing all rules and by going against all duty. The counter-rule is still a rule.

A critical reader will perhaps be surprised to see friendship and politeness regularly associated here, each distinguished, by a single trait, from ritualized behaviour. For whatever cultural tradition is linked to (Western or otherwise), the hypothesis about politeness and the sharp determination of this value relates to what enjoins us to go beyond rules, norms, and hence ritual. The internal contradiction in the concept of politeness, as in all normative concepts of which it would be an example, is that it involves both rules and invention without rule. Its rule is that one knows the rule but is never bound by it. It is impolite to be merely polite, to be polite out of politeness. We thus have here a rule—and this rule is recurrent, structural, general, that is to say, each time singular and exemplary —which commands action of such a sort that one not act simply by conformity to the normative rule but not even, by virtue of the said rule, out of respect for it.

Let's not beat around the bush [N'y allons pas par quatre chemins]: what is at issue is the concept of duty, and of knowing whether or up to what point one can rely on it, on what it structures in the order of culture, of morality, of politics, of law, and even of economy (especially as to the relation between debt and duty);[3] that is to say, whether and up to what point one can trust what the concept of duty lays down for all responsible discourse about responsible decisions, for all discourse, all logic, all rhetoric *of* responsibility. By speaking of responsible discourse on responsibility, we are *implying* already that discourse itself must submit to the norms or to the law of which it speaks. This implication would seem to be inescapable, but it remains disconcerting: what could be the responsibility, the quality or the virtue of responsibility, of a consistent discourse which claimed to show that no responsibility could ever be taken without equivocation and without contradiction? Or that the self-justification of a decision is impossible, and could not, a priori and for structural reasons, respond absolutely for itself?

We have just said: "*n'y allons pas par quatre chemins* [an almost untranslatable French expression which invokes the cross or the crucial, the crossing of ways, the four and the fork of a crossroad (*quadrifurcum*) in order to say: let us proceed directly, without detour, without ruse and without calculation]: *what is at issue* [il s'agit de] *is the concept of* . . . and *knowing whether* . . . ." What is implied by an expression of such an imperative order? That one could and one should tackle a concept or a problem frontally, in a nonoblique way. There would be a concept and a problem (of this or that, of duty, for example, it matters little for the moment), that is to say, something determinable by a knowing ("what matters is knowing whether") and that lies before you, there before you (*problema*), *in front of you* [in English in the original—Tr.]; from which comes the necessity to approach from the front, facing towards, in a way which is at once direct, frontal, and head on [*capitale*], what is before your eyes, your mouth, your hands (and not behind your back), there, before you, like an *object* pro-posed or posed in advance [*pro-posé ou pré-posé*], a question to deal with, therefore quite as much a *subject* proposed (that is to say, surren- dered, offered up: in principle one always offers from the front, surely? in principle). Continuing the semantics of *problema*, there would also be the question of an *ob-subject extended* like a jetty or the promontory of a headland [*cap*],[4] an armor, or protective garment. *Problema* also means, in certain contexts, the excuse given in advance to shirk or clear oneself of blame, but also something else that would perhaps interest us here more. By metonymy, if you will, *problema* can come to designate that which, as we say in French, serves as a "cover" when assuming responsibility for an- other or passing oneself off as the other, or while speaking in the name of the other, that which one places before one or behind which one hides. Think of the passion of Philoctetus, of Ulysses the oblique—and of the third (*terstis*), at once innocent witness (*testis*), *actor*-participant but also an *actor* to whom it is given to play a role, instrument and active delegate *by representation*, that is the *prob- lematic* child, Neoptolemus.[5] From this point of view responsibility would be *problematic* to the further [*supplementaire*] extent that it could sometimes, perhaps even always, be what one takes, not for oneself, *in one's own name* and *before the other* (the most classically metaphysical definition of responsibility) but what one must take for another, in his place, in the name of the other or of oneself as other, before another other, and an other of the other, namely the very undeniable of ethics. "To the further [*supplementaire*] extent," we said, but we must go further: in the degree to which responsibility not only fails to weaken but on the contrary arises in a structure which is itself supplementary. It is always exercised in my name *as* the name of the other, and that in no way affects its singularity. This singularity is posited and must quake in the exemplary equivocality and insecurity of this "as."

If the experience of responsibility could not be reduced to one of duty or of debt, if the "response" of responsibility no longer appeared in a concept with respect to which we must "know whether . . ."; if all this were to challenge the space of the *problem* and returned not only to within the pro-positional form of the response but even to within the "*question*" form of thought or language, and thus what is no longer or not yet problematic or questionable, i.e., critique, namely of the order of judicative decision, we could no longer, we *should not above all* approach in a direct, frontal *projective*, that is, thetic or thematic way. And this "do not do it," this "should not above all," which seems to give the slip to the problem, the project, the question, the theme, the thesis, the critique, would have nothing to do with a shortcoming, a lapse in logical or demonstrative rigor, quite the contrary (always supposing that the imperative of rigor, *stricto sensu*, of the most *strict* rigor, is sheltered from all questioning[6]). If there was a shortcoming, and a shortcoming of justice as much as of reading, it would occur rather on the side where one would want to summon such a "do-not-do-it," a "should-not-above-all-do-it," to appear before some philosophical or moral tribunal, that is to say, before proceedings both critical and juridical. Nothing would seem more violent or naive than to call for more frontality, more thesis or more thematization, to suppose that one can find a standard here. How can one choose between the economy or the discretion of the *ellipse* with which one credits a writing, and an *a-thematicity*, an insufficiently thematic explanation of which some believe it is possible to accuse a philosopher?

II

Instead of tackling the question or the problem head on, directly, straightforwardly, which would doubtless be impossible, inappropriate, or illegitimate, should we proceed obliquely? I have often done so, even to the point of demanding obliqueness by name[7] even while acknowledging it, some might think, as a failure of duty since the figure of the oblique is often associated with lack of frankness or of directness. It is doubtless with this fatality in mind, this tradition of the oblique in which I am in some way inscribed, that David Wood, in order to invite me, encourage me, or oblige me to contribute to this volume, suggests to me [*m'offre*] that these pages be entitled "An Oblique Offering." He had even printed it beforehand on the projected Table of Contents of the complete manuscript before I had written a line of this text.[8] Will we ever know whether this "offering" is mine or his? Who takes responsibility for it? This question is as serious and intractable [*intraitable*][9] as the responsibility for the name one is given or bears, for the name that one receives or the name that one gives oneself. The infinite paradoxes of what is so calmly called narcissism are outlined here: suppose that X, something or someone (a trace, a work, an institution, a child), bears your name, that is to say, your title. The naive rendering or common illusion [*fantasme courant*] is that you have given your name to X, thus all that returns to X, in a direct or indirect way, in a straight or oblique line, *returns* to you, as a profit for your narcissism. But as you *are* not your name, nor your title, and given that, as the name or the title, X does very well without you or your life, that is, without the place toward which something could *return*—just as that is the definition and the very possibility of every trace, and of all names and all titles, so your narcissism is frustrated a priori by that from which it profits or hopes to profit. Conversely, suppose that X did not want your name or your title; suppose that, for one reason or another, X broke free from it and chose himself another name, working a kind of repeated severance from the originary severance; then your narcissism, doubly injured, will find itself all the more enriched precisely *on account of this*: that which bears, has borne, will bear your name seems sufficiently free, powerful, creative, and autonomous to live alone and radically to do without you and your name. What returns to your name, to the secret of your name, is the ability to disappear *in your name.* And thus not to return to itself, which is the condition of the gift (for example, of the name) but also of all expansion of self, of all augmentation of self, of all *auctoritas.* In the two cases of this same divided passion, it is impossible to dissociate the greatest profit and the greatest privation. It is consequently impossible to construct a noncontradictory or coherent concept of narcissism, thus to give a univocal sense to the "I." It is impossible to speak it or to act it, as "I," and as Baudelaire put it, *sans façon* [without ado; without ceremony]. This is the secret of the bow or of the instrumental string (*neura*) for Philoctetus, for the passion according to Philoctetus: the child is the problem, always, that is the truth.

On reflection, the oblique does not seem to me to offer the best figure for all the moves that I have tried to describe in that way. I have always been ill at ease with this word of which I have, however, so often made use. Even if I have done so in a generally negative way, to disrupt rather than to prescribe, to avoid or to say that one ought to avoid, that moreover one could not fail to avoid defiance or direct confrontation, the immediate approach. Confession or auto-critique, then: one has to smile at the hypothesis of the most hyperbolic *hybris,* namely the hypothesis that this whole "critical reader" would add up to an "autocritical reader" (critique of self, but critique of whom exactly? To whom would the reflexive be returned?), a reader that sustains itself and carries itself along, having in particular no more need of "me" for this purpose, no need of an I which itself needs no help from anyone else in asking itself all the questions or putting to itself all the critical objections that one could want. (In the syntax of "X: A Critical Reader," it will, moreover, always be difficult to determine who is the reader of whom, who the subject, who the text, who the object, and who offers what—or whom—to whom.) What one would have to criticize in the oblique, today, is without doubt the geometrical figure, the compromise still made with the primitiveness of the plane, the line, the angle, the diagonal, and thus of the right angle between the vertical and the horizontal. The oblique remains the choice of a strategy that is still crude, obliged to ward off what is most urgent, a geometric calculus for diverting as quickly as possible both the frontal approach and the straight line: presumed to be the shortest path from one point to another. Even in its rhetorical form and in the figure of figure that is called *oratio obliqua*, this displacement still appears too direct, linear, in short, economic, in complicity with the diagonal arc. (I think straightaway of the fact that a bow [*arc*] is sometimes *stretched*; and again of the passion of Philoctetus; to say of a bow [*arc*] that it is stretched [*tendu*] can mean, in some contexts, that its string is taut and ready to propel the weapon, namely, the deadly arrow, or that the bow is offered [up], given, delivered, transmitted (*handed on, over to* [English in original—Tr.]). Let us therefore forget the oblique.

Is this a way of not responding to the invitation of David Wood and of all those whom he represents here? Ought I to respond to him? How is one to know? What is an invitation? What is it to respond to an invitation? To whom, to what, does this return, what does it amount to? [*à quoi cela revient-il?*]. An invitation leaves one free, otherwise it becomes constraint. It should [*devrait*] never imply: you are obliged to come, you have to come, it is necessary. But the invitation must be pressing, not indifferent. It should never imply: you are free not to come and if you don't come, never mind, it doesn't matter. Without the pressure of some desire—which at once says "come" and leaves, nevertheless, the other his absolute freedom—the invitation immediately withdraws and becomes unwelcoming. It must therefore split and redouble itself at the same time, at once leave free and take hostage: double act, redoubled act. Is an invitation possible? We have just glimpsed under what conditions there would be an invitation, if there is one, but even if there is one, does it ever present itself, in fact, as such, at the moment?

What we are glimpsing of the invitation (but of the call in general, as well) governs by the same "token" the logic of the response, both of the response to the invitation and the response by itself.

Whoever ponders the necessity, the genealogy and therefore also the limits of the concept of responsibility cannot fail to wonder at some point what is meant by "respond," and *responsiveness* [English in original—Tr.], a precious word for which I can find no strict equivalent in my language. And to wonder whether "to respond" has an opposite, which would consist, if commonsense is to be believed, in not responding. Is it possible to make a decision on the subject of "responding" and of "responsiveness"?

One can today, in many different places, attend to or participate in a congenial and disturbing task: restoring morality and, especially, reassuring those who had serious reasons for being troubled by this topic. Some souls believe themselves to have found in Deconstruction [*"la" Déconstruction*]—as if there were one, and only one—a modern form of immorality, of amorality, or of irresponsibility (etc.: a discourse too well known; I do not need to continue), while others, more serious, in less of a hurry, better disposed toward so-called Deconstruction, today claim the opposite; they discern encouraging signs and in increasing numbers (at times, I must admit, in some of my texts) which would testify to a permanent, extreme, direct, or oblique, in any event, increasingly intense attention, to those things which one could identify under the fine names of "ethics," "morality," "responsibility," "subject," etc. Before reverting to not-responding, it would be necessary to declare in the most direct way that if one had the *sense* of duty and of responsibility, it would compel breaking with both these moralisms, with these two restorations of morality, including, therefore, the remoralization of deconstruction, which naturally seems more attractive than that to which it is rightly opposed, but which at each moment risks reassuring itself in order to reassure the other and to promote the consensus of a new dogmatic slumber. And it is so that one not be in too much of a hurry to say that it is in the name of a *higher* responsibility and a more intractable [*intraitable*] moral exigency that one declares one's distaste, uneven as it may be, for both moralisms. Undoubtedly, it is always following the affirmation of a certain excess that one can suspect the well-known immorality, indeed the denigrating hypocrisy of moralisms. But nothing allows one to assert that the best names or the most suitable figures for this affirmation are ethics, morality, politics, responsibility, or the subject. Furthermore, would it be moral and responsible to act morally because one has a *sense* (the word emphasized above) of duty and responsibility? Clearly not; it would be too easy and, precisely, natural, programmed by nature: it is hardly moral to be moral (responsible, etc.) because one has the *sense* of the moral, of the highness of the law, etc. This is the well-known problem of "respect" for the moral law, itself the "cause" of respect in the Kantian sense; this problem draws all of its interest from the disturbing paradox that it inscribes in the heart of a morality incapable of giving an account of being inscribed in an affect (*Gefühl*) or in a sensibility of what should not be inscribed there or should only enjoin the sacrifice of everything that would only obey this sensible inclination. It is well known that sacrifice and the sacrificial offering are at the heart of Kantian morality, under their own name (*Opferung, Aufopferung*). (Cf., for example, Kant's *Critique of Practical Reason*, L. 1, ch. III. The object of sacrifice there is always of the order of the sensuous motives [*mobile sensible*], of the secretly "pathological" interest which must, says Kant, be "humbled" before the moral law; this concept of sacrificial offering, thus of sacrifice in general, requires the whole apparatus of the "critical" distinctions of Kantianism: sensible/intelligible, passivity/spontaneity, *intuitus derivativus / intuitus originarius*, etc.; the same goes for the concept of *passion*; what I am looking for here, passion according to me, would be a concept of passion that would be non-"pathological" in Kant's sense.)

All this, therefore, still remains open, suspended, undecided, questionable even beyond the question, indeed, to make use of another figure, absolutely aporetic. What is the ethicity of ethics? The morality of morality? What is responsibility? What is the "What is?" in this case? etc. These questions are always urgent. In a certain way they must remain urgent and unanswered, at any rate without a general and rule-governed response, without a response other than that which is linked specifically each time, to the occurrence of a decision without rules and without will in the course of a new test of the undecidable. And let it not be said too precipitately that these questions or these propositions are *already* inspired by a concern that could by right be called ethical, moral, responsible, etc. For sure, in saying that ("And let it not be said too precipitately . . ." etc.), one gives ammunition to the officials of anti-deconstruction, but all in all isn't that preferable to the constitution of a consensual euphoria or, worse, a community of complacent deconstructionists, reassured and reconciled with the world in ethical certainty, good conscience, satisfaction of service rendered, and the consciousness of duty accomplished (or, more heroically still, yet to be accomplished)?

So the nonresponse. Clearly, it will always be possible to say, and it will be true, that nonresponse is a response. One always has, one always must have, the right not to respond, and this liberty belongs to responsibility itself, that is, to the liberty that one believes must be associated with it. One must always be free not to respond to an appeal or to an invitation—and it is worth remembering this, reminding oneself of the essence of this liberty. Those who think that responsibility or the sense of responsibility is a good thing, a prime virtue, indeed the Good itself, are convinced, however, that one must always answer (for oneself, to the other, before the other, or before the law) and that, moreover, a nonresponse is always a modality determined in the space opened by an unavoidable responsibility. Is there then nothing more to say about nonresponse? On it or on the subject of it, if not in its favor?

Let us press on and, in the attempt to convince more quickly, let us take an example, whether or not it is valid for the law. What example? This one. And certainly, when I say this very example, I already say something more and something else; I say something which goes beyond the *tode ti*, the this of the example. The example itself, as such, overflows its singularity as much as its identity. This is why there are no examples, while at the same time there are only examples; I have said this, too, often about many examples, no doubt. The exemplarity of the example is clearly never the exem-

plarity of the example. We can never be sure of having put an end
to this very old children's game in which all the discourses, philosophical or not, which have ever inspired deconstructions are
entangled by the performative fiction which consists in saying,
starting up the game again, "take precisely this example."

If, for example, I respond to the invitation which is made to me
to respond to the texts collected here, which do me the honour or
the kindness [*l'amitié*] of taking an interest in certain of my earlier
publications, am I not going to be heaping up errors [*fautes*] and
therefore conduct myself in an irresponsible way—by taking on
false [*mauvaises*] responsibilities? What faults?

1. First of all, that of endorsing a situation, of subscribing to it
and acting as if I found myself at ease in such a strange place, as if I
found it normal or natural to speak here, as if we were sitting down
at the table in the midst of twelve people who were speaking on the
whole about "me" or addressing themselves to "me." "I" [*Moi*],
who am both a twelfth insofar as I am part of a group, one among
others, and already, being thus split or redoubled, the thirteenth
insofar as I am not one example among others in the series of
twelve. What would it look like if I supposed I could reply to all
these men and this woman at the same time, or if I supposed I
could *begin by responding*, thus disregarding the very scholarly and
very singular strategy of each of these eleven or twelve discourses, at
once so generous and so unself-satisfied and so overdetermined? By
speaking last, both in conclusion and in introduction, in twelfth or
thirteenth place, am I not taking the insane risk and adopting the
odious attitude of treating all these thinkers as disciples, indeed the
apostles, among whom some would be preferred by me, others
potential evil traitors? Who would be Judas here? What is someone
to do who does not want to be and who knows himself not to be
(but how can one be sure about these things, and how can one
extricate oneself from these matrices?) either an apostle (*apostolos*, a
messenger of God), or Jesus, or Judas? Because it dawned on me a
little late, counting the number of participants gathered here,
exactly twelve (who is still to come?), then noticing the words

"oblique offering" and "passion" in his letter, that David Wood was perhaps the perverse producer [*metteur en scène*] of a mystery—and that in fact the "oblique offering," which was no less his than mine, had a flavor that was ironically, sarcastically, eucharistic (no vegetarian—there are at least two among the guests—will ever be able to break with the sublimity of mystical cannibalism): the "this is my body which is given for you, keep this in remembrance of me," is this not the most oblique offering [*don*]? Is this not what I commented on all year long in *Glas* or in my last seminars on "eating—the other" and the "rhetoric of cannibalism"? All the more reason not to respond. This is no Last Supper [*Cène*], and the ironic friendship which brings us together consists in knowing this, while peering with a "squinty eye" [English in original—Tr.] toward this cannibalism in mourning.

2. If I did respond I would put myself in the situation of someone who felt *capable of responding*: he has an answer for everything, he takes himself to be up to answering each of us, each question, each objection or criticism; he does not see that each of the texts gathered here has its force, its logic, its singular strategy, that it would be necessary to reread everything, to reconstitute the work and its trajectory, the themes and arguments of each, the discursive tradition and the many texts set to work, etc. To claim to do all this, and to do it in a few pages, would smack of a *hybris* and a naïveté without limit—and from the outset a flagrant lack of respect for the discourse, the work, and the offering of the other. More reasons for not responding.

3. From these two arguments we can glimpse that a certain *nonresponse* can attest to this politeness (without rules) of which we spoke above, and finally to respect for others, that is to say, also to an exigency of responsibility. It will perhaps be said that this nonresponse is the best response, that it is still a response and a sign of responsibility. Perhaps. Let us wait and see. In any case, one thinks of that pride, that self-satisfaction, that elementary confidence which it would take to answer when a good education

teaches children that they must not "answer back" (at any rate in the sense and tradition of French manners) when grown-ups speak to them, they must not reproach them or criticize them, and certainly not ask them questions.

4. The overweening presumption from which *no response will ever be free* not only has to do with the fact that the response claims to measure up to the discourse of the other, to situate it, understand it, indeed circumscribe it by responding thus *to* the other and *before* the other. The respondent presumes, with as much frivolity as arrogance, that he can respond to the other and before the other because first of all he is able to answer for himself and for all he has been able to do, say, or write. To answer for oneself would here be to presume to know all that one could do, say, or write, to gather it together in an intelligible and coherent synthesis, to stamp it with one and the same seal (whatever the genre, the place, or the date, the discursive form, the contextual strategy, etc.), to posit that the same "I think" accompanies all "my" representations, which themselves form a systematic, homogeneous tissue of "theses," "themes," "objects," of "narratives," of "critiques," or of "evaluations," a tissue which can be subjectivized and of which I would have a total and intact memory, would know all the premises and all the consequences, etc.; this would also be to suppose that deconstruction is of the same order as the critique whose concept and history it precisely deconstructs. So many dogmatic naïvetés that one will never discourage, but all the more reason not to respond, not to act as if one could respond to the other, before the other, and for oneself. Someone will retort: indeed, but then this nonresponse is still a response, the most polite, the most modest, the most vigilant, the most respectful—both of the other and of truth. This nonresponse would again be a respectable form of politeness and respect, a responsible form of the vigilant exercise of responsibility. In any case, this would confirm that one cannot or that one ought not fail to respond. One cannot, one ought not to respond with nothing. The ought and the can are here strangely co-implicated. Perhaps. Let us wait and see.

Continuing these four preceding arguments, I would avoid errors (errors of politeness, moral errors, etc.) by not responding, by responding elliptically, by responding obliquely. I would have said to myself: it would be better, it is fairer, it is more decent, and more moral, not to respond. It is more respectful to the other, more responsible in the face of the imperative of critical, hypercritical, and above all "deconstructive" thought which insists on yielding as little as possible to dogmas and presuppositions. So you see—if I took heed of all these reasons, and if, still believing that this nonresponse was the best response, I decided not to respond, then I would run even worse risks.

Which ones?

1. To start with, the first injury or injustice: seeming not to take sufficiently seriously the persons and the texts offered here, to evince toward them an inadmissible ingratitude and a culpable indifference.

2. And then to exploit the "good reasons" for not responding to make use of silence in a way that is still strategic: because there is an art of the nonresponse, or of the deferred response, which is a rhetoric of war, a polemical ruse. Polite silence can become the most insolent weapon and the most deadly irony. On the pretext of waiting to have read through, pondered, labored to be able to begin to reply seriously (which will in fact be necessary and which could take forever), nonresponse as postponed or elusive, indeed absolutely elliptical response can always shelter one comfortably, safe from all objection. And on the pretext of feeling incapable of responding *to* the other, and answering *for* oneself, does one not undermine, both theoretically and practically, the concept of responsibility, which is actually the very essence of the *socius*?

3. To justify one's nonresponse by all these arguments, one can still refer to rules, to general norms, but then one falls short of the principle of politeness and of responsibility that we recalled above: never to believe oneself free of any debt and hence never to act

simply according to a rule, in conformity to duty not even *out of duty*, still less "out of politeness." Nothing would be more immoral and more impolite.

4. Certainly, nothing would be worse than substituting for an inadequate response, but one still giving evidence of a sincere, modest, finite, resigned effort, an interminable discourse. Such a discourse would pretend to provide, instead of a response or a nonresponse, a performative (more or less *performante* [literally: performing, also dynamic, effective] and more or less metalinguistic) for all these questions, nonquestions, or nonresponses. Such an operation would be open to the most justified critiques, it would offer its body, it would surrender, as if in sacrifice, the most vulnerable body to the most just blows. Because it would suffer from a *double* failure, it would combine two apparently contradictory faults: first, the claim to mastery or to an overview [*survol*] (be it meta-linguistic, meta-logical, meta-metaphysical, etc.) and second, the becoming-work of art (literary performance or performative, fiction, work), the aestheticizing play of a discourse from which one expects a serious, thoughtful, or philosophical response.

III

So, what are we to do? It is impossible to respond here. It is impossible to respond to this question about the response. It is impossible to respond to the question by which we precisely ask ourselves whether it is necessary to respond or not to respond, whether it is necessary, possible, or impossible. This aporia without end paralyzes us because it binds us doubly. (I must and I need not, I must not, it is necessary and impossible, etc.) In one and the same place, on the same apparatus, I have my two hands tied or nailed down. What are we to do? But also how is it that it does not prevent us from speaking, from continuing to describe the situation, from trying to make oneself understood? What is the nature of this language, since already it no longer belongs, no longer belongs simply, either to the question or to the response whose limits we have just verified and are continuing to verify? Of what does this verification consist, when nothing happens without some sacrifice? Will one call this a testimony [*témoignage*, also the act of "bearing witness"—Ed.] in a sense that neither the martyr, the attestation nor the testament would exhaust? And, as with every testimony, providing that it never be reducible, precisely, to verification, to proof or to demonstration, in a word, to knowledge?

Among other things, to return to the start of the scene, we find that the analyst, the one to whom we have given the name, can no longer describe or objectify the programmed development of a ritual, still less of a sacrificial offering. No one wanted to play the role of the sacrificeable or of the sacrificer, all the *agents* (priests, victims, participants, spectators, readers) not only *refuse to act*, but even if they wanted to make the prescribed gestures they would find themselves brought to a halt when faced with these contradictory orders. And it is not only a religious sociality whose identity is thus menaced, it is a philosophical sociality, insofar as it presupposes the order (preferably circular) of the appeal [or the call: *appel*—Tr.], of the question and the response. Some will say that this is the very principle of the community which sees itself thus exposed to disruption. Others will say that the threat of disruption threatens nothing, that it has always been the instituting or constitutive origin of religious or philosophical ties, of the social bond in general: the community lives and feeds on this vulnerability, and so it should. If the analyst in fact discovers limits to his work of scientific objectification, that is quite normal: he is a participant in a process which he would like to analyze, he can virtually play all the roles in it (that is to say, also mime them).[10] This limit furnishes positively the condition of his intelligence, of his reading, of his interpretations. But what would be the condition of this condition? The fact that the *Critical Reader* [English in original—Tr.] is a priori and endlessly exposed to a *critical reading* [English in original—Tr.].

What could escape this sacrificial verification and so secure the very space of *this very discourse, for example*? No question, no response, no responsibility. Let us say that there is a secret here. Let us testify: *There is something secret.* [*Il y a là du secret.*] We will leave the matter here for today, but not without an exercise on the essence and existence of such a secret, an exercise that will have an apophatic aspect.[11] The apophatic is not here necessarily dependent on negative theology, even if it makes it possible, too. And what we are attempting to put to the test is the possibility, in truth the impossibility, for any testimony to guarantee itself by expressing itself [*s'énonçant*] in the following form and grammar: "Let us testify that . . ."

We testify [*témoignons*] to a secret that is without content, without a content separable from its performative experience, from its performative tracing. (We shall not say from its performative *enunciation* or from its *propositional argumentation*; and we keep in reserve a number of questions about performativity in general.)

Let us say, therefore: *There is something secret* [*il y a là du secret*]. It would not be a matter of an artistic or technical secret reserved for someone—or for several, such as style, ruse, the signature of talent or the mark of a genius, the know-how that is thought to be incommunicable, untransmittable, unteachable, inimitable. It would not even be a matter of that psycho-physical secret, the art hidden in the depths of the human soul, of which Kant speaks in connection with the transcendental schematism, and of the imagination (*eine verborgene Kunst in den Tiefen der menschlichen Seele*).

There is something secret. It would not be a question of a secret as a representation dissimulated by a conscious subject, nor, moreover, of the content of an unconscious representation, some secret or mysterious motive that the moralist[12] or the psychoanalyst might have the skill to detect, or, as they say, to de-mystify. This secret would not even be of the order of absolute subjectivity, in the rather unorthodox sense, with respect to a history of metaphysics, that Kierkegaard gave to *existence* and to all that resists the concept or frustrates the system, especially the Hegelian dialectic. This secret would not belong to any of the stages (aesthetic, ethical, religious a or b) that Kierkegaard distinguishes. It would be neither sacred nor profane.

There is something secret. But to take account of what we have just suggested, the being-there of the secret belongs no more to the private than to the public. It is not a deprived interiority that one would have to reveal, confess, announce, that is, to which one would have to respond by accounting for it and thematizing it in broad daylight. Who would ever determine the proper extent of a thematization so as to judge it finally adequate? And is there any worse violence than that which consists in calling for the response, demanding that one *give an account of* everything, and preferably *thematically*? Because this secret is not phenomenalizable. Neither phenomenal nor noumenal. No more than religion, can philosophy, morality, politics, or the law accept the unconditional respect of this secret. These authorities are constituted as authorities who may properly ask for accounts, that is, responses, from those with accepted responsibilities. No doubt they allow sometimes that there are conditional secrets (the secret of confession, the professional secret, the military secret, the manufacturing secret, the state secret). But the *right to secrets* is in all these cases a conditional right. Because the secret can be shared there, and limited by given conditions. The secret becomes simply a *problem*. It can and must be made known under other circumstances. Everywhere that a response and a responsibility are required, the right to a secret becomes conditional. There are no secrets, only problems for the knowledges which in this respect include not only philosophy, science, and technology, but also religion, morality, politics, and the law.

There is something secret. [*Il y a du secret.*] It concerns neither that into which a revealed religion *initiates* us nor that which it *reveals* (namely a mystery of passion), nor a learned ignorance (in a Christian brotherhood practicing a kind of negative theology), nor the content of an esoteric doctrine (for example, in a Pythagorean,

Platonic, or neo-Platonic community). In any case it cannot be reduced to these because it makes them possible. The secret is not mystical.

There is something secret. But it does not conceal itself. Heterogeneous to the hidden, to the obscure, to the nocturnal, to the invisible, to what can be dissimulated and indeed to what is nonmanifest in general, it cannot be unveiled. It remains inviolable even when one thinks one has revealed it. Not that it hides itself forever in an indecipherable crypt or behind an absolute veil. It simply exceeds the play of veiling/unveiling, dissimulation/revelation, night/day, forgetting/anamnesis, earth/heaven, etc. It does not belong therefore to the truth, neither to the truth as *homoiosis* or adequation, nor to the truth as memory (Mnemosyne, *aletheia*), nor to the given truth, nor to the promised truth, nor to the inaccessible truth. Its nonphenomenality is without relation, even negative relation, to phenomenality. Its reserve is no longer of the intimacy that one likes to call secret, of the very close or very proper which sucks in or inspires [*aspires ou inspires*] so much profound discourse (the *Geheimnis* or, even richer, the inexhaustible *Unheimliche*).

Certainly, one could speak this secret in other names, whether one finds them or gives them to it. Moreover, this happens at every instant. It remains secret under all names and it is its irreducibility to the very name which makes it secret, even when one *makes the truth* in its name [*fait la verité à son sujet*] as Augustine put it so originally. The secret is that one here calls it secret, putting it for once in relation to all the secrets which bear the same name but cannot be reduced to it. The secret would also be homonymy, not so much a hidden resource of homonymy, but the functional possibility of homonymy or of *mimesis*.

There is something secret. One can always speak about it, that is not enough to disrupt it. One can speak of it ad infinitum, tell stories[13] about it, utter all the discourses which it puts to work and the stories which it unleashes or enchains, because the secret often makes one think of these secret histories and it even gives one a taste for them. And the secret will remain secret, mute, impassive as the *khōra*, as *Khōra* foreign to every history, as much in the sense of *Geschichte* or *res gestae* as of knowledge and of historical narrative (*epistémè, historia rerum gestarum*), and outside all periodization, all epochalization. It remains silent, not to keep a word in reserve or withdrawn [*en retrait*], but because it remains foreign to speech [*la parole*], without our even being able to say in that distinguished syntagm: "the secret is that in speech which is foreign to speech." It is no more in speech than foreign to speech. It does not answer to speech, it does not say "I, the secret," it does not correspond, it does not answer [*répondre*]: either for itself or to anyone else, before anyone or anything whatsoever. Absolute nonresponse which one could not even call to account or for something on account [*acomptes*], grant indemnities, excuses, or "discounts"—so many ruses, always, to draw it into a *process* [*procès*] that is philosophical, ethical, political, juridical, etc. The secret gives rise to no *process* [*procès*]. It may appear to give rise to one (indeed it always does so), it may lend itself to it, but it never surrenders to it. The ethics of the discussion may always not respect it (according to me it owes it respect, even if this seems difficult or contradictory, because the secret is intractable [*intraitable*]), but it will never reduce it. Moreover, no discussion would either begin or continue without it. And whether one respects it or not, the secret remains there impassively, at a distance, out of reach. In this one cannot not respect it, whether one likes it or not, whether one knows it or not.

There, there is no longer time nor place.

A confidence to end with today. Perhaps all I wanted to do was to confide or confirm my taste (probably unconditional) for literature, more precisely for literary writing. Not that I like literature in general, nor that I prefer it to something else, to philosophy, for example, as they suppose who ultimately discern neither one nor the other. Not that I want to reduce everything to it, especially not philosophy. Literature I could, fundamentally do without, in fact, rather easily. If I had to retire to an island, it would be particularly history books, memoirs, that I would doubtless take with me, and that I would read in my own way, perhaps to make literature out of them, unless it would be the other way round, and this would be true for other books (art, philosophy, religion, human or natural sciences, law, etc.). But if, without liking literature in general and for its own sake, I like something *about it*, which above all cannot be reduced to some aesthetic quality, to some source of formal pleasure [*jouissance*], this would be *in place of the secret*. In place of an absolute secret. There would be the passion. There is no passion without secret, this very secret, indeed no secret without this passion. *In place of the secret*: there where nevertheless everything is said and where what remains is nothing—but the remainder, not even of literature.

I have often found myself insisting on the necessity of distinguishing between literature and belles-lettres or poetry. Literature is a modern invention, inscribed in conventions and institutions which, to hold on to just this trait, secure in principle its *right to say everything*. Literature thus ties its destiny to a certain noncensure, to the space of democratic freedom (freedom of the press, freedom of speech, etc.). No democracy without literature; no literature without democracy. One can always want neither one nor the other, and there is no shortage of doing without them under all regimes; it is quite possible to consider neither of them to be unconditional goods and indispensable rights. But in no case can one dissociate one from the other. No analysis would be equal to it. And each time that a literary work is censured, democracy is in danger, as everyone agrees. The possibility of literature, the legitimation that a society gives it, the allaying of suspicion or terror with regard to it, all that goes together—politically—with the unlimited right to ask any question, to suspect all dogmatism, to analyze every presupposition, even those of the ethics or the politics of responsibility.

But this authorization to say everything paradoxically makes the author an author who is not responsible to anyone, not even to himself, for whatever the persons or the characters of his works, thus of what he is supposed to have written himself, say and do, for example. And these "voices" speak, allow or make to come—even in literatures without persons and without characters. This authorization to say everything (which goes together with democracy, as the apparent hyper-responsibility of a "subject") acknowledges a right to absolute nonresponse, just where there can be no question of responding, of being able to or having to respond. This nonresponse is more original and more secret than the modalities of power and duty because it is fundamentally heterogeneous to them. We find there a hyperbolic condition of democracy which seems to contradict a certain determined and historically limited concept of such a democracy, a concept which links it to the concept of a subject that is calculable, accountable, imputable, and responsible, a subject having-to-respond [*devant - repondre*], having-to-tell [*devant - dire*] the truth, having to testify according to the sworn word ("the whole truth, nothing but the truth"), before the law [*devant la loi*], having to reveal the secret, with the exception of certain situations that are determinable and regulated by law (confession, the professional secrets of the doctor, the psychoanalyst, or the lawyer, secrets of national defence or state secrets in general, manufacturing secrets, etc.). This contradiction also indicates the task (task of thought, also theoretico-practical task) for any democracy to come.

There is in literature, in the *exemplary* secret of literature, a chance of saying everything without touching upon the secret. When all hypotheses are permitted, groundless and ad infinitum, about the meaning of a text, or the final intentions of an author, whose person is no more represented than nonrepresented by a character or by a narrator,[14] by a poetic or fictional sentence, which detaches itself from its presumed source and thus remains *locked away* [*au secret*], when there is no longer even any sense in making decisions about some secret behind the surface of a textual manifestation (and it is this situation which I would call text or trace), when it is the call [*appel*] of this secret, however, which points back to the other or to something else, when it is this itself which keeps our passion aroused, and holds us to the other, then the secret impassions us. Even if there is none, even if it does not exist, hidden behind anything whatever. Even if the secret is no secret, even if there has never been a secret, a single secret. Not one.

Can one ever finish with obliqueness? The secret, if there is one, is not hidden at the corner of an angle, it does not lay itself open to a double view or to a squinting gaze. It cannot be seen, quite simply. No more than a word. As soon as there are words—and this can be said of the trace in general, and of the chance that it is— direct intuition no longer has any chance. One can reject, as we have done, the word "oblique"; one cannot deny the destinerrant indirection [*indirection destinerrante*: see Derrida's *The Post Card: From Socrates to Freud and Beyond*, trans. Alan Bass (Chicago: University of Chicago Press, 1987)—Tr.] as soon as there is a trace. Or, if you prefer, one can only deny it.

One can stop and examine [*arraisonner*] a secret, make it say things, make out that [*donner à croire*] there is something there when there is not. One can lie, cheat, seduce by making use of it. One can play with the secret as with a simulacrum, with a lure or yet another strategy. One can cite it as an impregnable resource. One can try in this way to secure for oneself a phantasmatic power over others. That happens every day. But this very simulacrum still bears witness to a possibility which exceeds it. It does not exceed it in the direction of some ideal community, rather toward a solitude without any measure common to that of an isolated subject, a so- lipsism of the *ego* whose sphere of belonging (*Eigentlichkeit*) would give rise [*lieu*] to some analogical appresentation of the alter ego and to some genesis constitutive of intersubjectivity (Husserl), or with that of a *Jemeinigkeit* of *Dasein* whose solitude, Heidegger tells us, is still a modality of *Mitsein*. Solitude, the other name of the secret to which the simulacrum still bears witness, is neither of consciousness, nor of the subject, nor of *Dasein*, not even of *Dasein* in its authentic being-able, whose testimony or attestation (*Be- zeugung*) Heidegger analyzes (cf. *Being and Time*, par. 54ff). It makes them possible, but what it makes possible does not put an end to the secret. The secret never allows itself to be captured or covered over by the relation to the other, by being-with or by any form of "social bond". Even if it makes them possible, it does not answer to them, it is what does not answer. No *responsiveness* [English in original—Tr.]. Shall we call this death? Death dealt? Death dealing? I see no reason not to call that life, existence, trace. And it is not the contrary.

Consequently, if the simulacrum still bears witness to a possibility which exceeds it, this exceeding remains, it (is) *the* remainder, and it remains such [*il (est)* le *reste*, il le rest] even if one precisely cannot here trust any definite witness, nor even any guaranteed value to bearing witness, or, to put it another way, as the name suggests, to the history of any *martyrdom* (*martyria*). For one will never reconcile the value of a testimony with that of knowledge or of certainty—it is impossible and it ought not be done. One will never reduce the one to the other—it is impossible and it ought not be done.

That remains, according to me, the absolute solitude of a passion without martyrdom.

TRANSLATED BY DAVID WOOD

SAUF LE NOM

NOTE: The first version of this text was published in English under the title *Post-Scriptum* (subtitle: *Aporias, Ways and Voices*) in a volume devoted to negative theology (Harold Coward and Toby Foshay, eds., *Derrida and Negative Theology* [Albany: State University of New York Press, 1992]). I had been invited to respond, in the form of a conclusion, to the papers delivered at a conference having the same title as the volume, organized under the auspices of the Calgary Institute for the Humanities in Canada, and under the direction of Harold Coward. I was not able to attend this colloquium. This fictive dialogue was written, therefore, after reading the papers, themselves gathered in the volume mentioned above. I would like to thank again the authors: Toby Foshay, Michel Despland, Mark C. Taylor, Harold Coward, David Loy, and Morny Joy. In order to reconstitute a context, the editors of that volume republished in English translations two essays that I had already brought out elsewhere, *D'un ton apocalyptique adopté naguère en philosophie* (Paris: Galilée, 1983), "Of an Apocalyptic Tone Recently Adopted in Philosophy," trans. John P. Leavey, Jr., *The Oxford Literary Review* 6: 2 (1984); and "Comment ne pas parler: Dénegations," in *Psyché: Inventions de l'autre* (Paris: Galilée, 1987), "How to Avoid Speaking: Denials," trans. Ken Frieden, in Sanford Budick and Wolfgang Iser, eds., *Languages of the Unsayable: The Play of Negativity in Literature and Literary Theory* (New York: Columbia University Press, 1989), pp. 3–70.

§ Sauf le nom
(Post-Scriptum)

— . . .

—Sorry, but more than one, it is always necessary to be more than one in order to speak, several voices are necessary for that . . .

—Yes, granted, and par excellence, let us say exemplarily, when it's a matter of God . . .

—Still more, if this is possible, when one claims to speak about God according to what they call apophasis [*l'apophase*], in other words, according to the voiceless voice [*la voix blanche*], the way of theology called or so-called negative. This voice multiplies itself, dividing within itself: it says one thing and its contrary, God that is without being or God that (is) beyond being. The *apophasis* is a declaration, an explanation, a response that, taking on the subject of God a negative or interrogative form (for that is also what *apophasis* means), at times so resembles a profession of atheism as to be mistaken for it. All the more because the modality of *apophasis*, despite its negative or interrogative value, often recalls that of the sentence, verdict, or decision, of the *statement* [in English in the original—Ed.]. I would like to speak to you, don't hesitate to interrupt me, of this multiplicity of voices, of this quite initial, but interminable as well, end of monologism—and of what follows . . .

35

—Like a certain mysticism, apophatic discourse has always been suspected of atheism. Nothing seems at once more merited and more insignificant, more displaced, more blind than such a trial [*procès*]. Leibniz himself was inclined to this. Heidegger recalls what he said of Angelus Silesius: "With every mystic there are some places that are extraordinarily bold, full of difficult metaphors and inclining almost to Godlessness, just as I have seen in the German poems of a certain Angelus Silesius, poems beautiful besides."[1]

Inclining, but not going beyond incline or inclination, not even or almost (*beinahe zur Gottlosigkeit hinneigend*), and the oblique slope [*penchant*] of this *clinamen* does not seem separable from a certain boldness of language [*langue*], from a poetic or metaphoric tongue . . .

—And beautiful besides, don't forget, Leibniz notes this as if it were a matter of an addition or an accessory (*im übrigen schönen Gedichten*), but I wonder if it isn't a matter there, beauty or sublimity, of an essential trait of negative theology. As for the example of Angelus Silesius . . .

—Let's leave this question aside for the moment: does the *heritage* of Angelus Silesius (Johannes Scheffler) belong to the tradition of negative theology in the strict sense or not? Can one speak here of a "strict sense"? You couldn't deny, I think, that Angelus Silesius keeps an evident kinship with apophatic theology. His example signifies for us, at this moment, only this affinity between the atheism suspected by Leibniz and a certain apophatic boldness. This apophatic boldness always consists in going further than is reasonably permitted. That is one of the essential traits of all negative theology: passing to the limit, then crossing a frontier, including that of a community, thus of a sociopolitical, institutional, ecclesial reason or raison d'être.

—If on the one hand apophasis inclines almost toward atheism, can't one say that, on the other hand or thereby, the extreme and most consequent forms of declared atheism will have always testified [*témoigné*] to the most intense desire of God? Isn't that from then on a program or a matrix? A typical and identifiable recurrence?

—Yes and no. There is one apophasis that can in effect respond to, correspond to, correspond with the most insatiable *desire of God*, according to the history and the event of its manifestation or the secret of its nonmanifestation. The other apophasis, the other voice, can remain readily foreign to all desire, in any case to every anthropotheomorphic form of desire.

—But isn't it proper to desire to carry with it its own proper suspension, the death or the phantom of desire? To go toward the absolute other, isn't that the extreme tension of a desire that tries thereby to renounce its own proper momentum, its own movement of appropriation?

—To testify, you were saying, to testify to the desire *of* God. The phrase is not only equivocal, of an equivocity essential, signifying, decisive in its very undecidability, to wit, the equivocity that the double genitive marks ("objective" and "subjective," even before the grammatical or ontological upsurge of a subject or an object), in other words, the equivocity of the origin and of the end of such a desire: does it come from God in us, from God for us, from us for God? And as we do not determine *ourselves before* this desire, as no relation to self can be sure of preceding it, to wit, of preceding a relation to the other, even were this to be through mourning, all reflection is caught in the genealogy of this genitive. I understand by that a reflection on self, an autobiographical reflection, for example, as well as a reflection on the idea or on the name of God. But your phrase is otherwise equivocal: when it names *testimony*. For if atheism, like aphophatic theology, testifies to the desire of God, if it avows, confesses, or indirectly signifies, as in a symptom, the desire of God, in the presence of whom does it do this? Who speaks to whom? Let us stay a little while with this question and feign to know what a discourse of negative theology is, with its determined traits and its own proper inclination. To whom is this discourse addressed? Who is its addressee? Does it exist before this

interlocutor, before the discourse, before its actualization [*son passage à l'acte*], before its performative accomplishment? Dionysius
the Areopagite, for example, articulates a certain prayer, turned
toward God; he links it with an address to the disciple, more
precisely to the becoming-disciple of him who is thus called to
hear. An apostrophe (to God) is turned toward another apostrophe
in the direction of him . . .

—Never of her . . .

—Not to my knowledge, not in this case (but don't hasten to
conclude that the scene is unfolding between men, and above all
that the one who speaks is a man). The other apostrophe is thus
addressed to him who, precisely, does not yet know what he knows
or should know, but should know with a nonknowledge, according
to a certain nonknowledge. The hymn and the didactic become
allied here according to a mode whose essential and thus irreducible originality would have to be recaptured. It is a matter of a
singular movement of the soul or, if you prefer, of a conversion of
existence that accords itself to, in order to reveal in its very night,
the most secret secret. This conversion turns (itself) toward the
other in order to turn (it) toward God, without there being an
order to these two movements that are in truth the same, without
one or the other being circumvented or diverted. Such a conversion
is no doubt not without relation to the movement of the Augustinian confession . . .

—Whose autobiographical character and what that confession
inaugurates in this regard it would also be useless to recall; it would
be naive to think that one knows what is the essence, the provenance, or the history of autobiography outside events like Augustine's *Confessions* . . .

—When he asks (himself), when he asks in truth of God and
already of his readers why he confesses himself to God when He
knows everything, the response makes it appear that what is essen-

tial to the avowal or the testimony does not consist in an experience of knowledge. Its act is not reduced to informing, teaching, making known. Stranger to knowing, thus to every determination or to every predicative attribution, confession shares [*partage*] this destiny with the apophatic movement. Augustine's response is inscribed from the outset in the Christian order of love or charity: as fraternity. In order to make them better in charity, Augustine addresses himself to "brotherly and devout ears" (10.34.51), and to the "brotherly mind" so that it "loves in me" what you, God, "teach us to love" (*Amet in me fraternus animus quod amandum doces*) (10.4.6). Confession does not consist in making known—and thereby it teaches that teaching as the transmission of positive knowledge is not essential. The avowal does not belong in essence to the order of cognitive determination; it is quasi-apophatic in this regard. It has nothing to do with knowledge—with knowledge as such. As act of charity, love, and friendship in Christ, the avowal is destined to God and to creatures, to the Father and to the brothers in order to "stir up" love, to augment an affect, love, among them, among us (11.1.1). And so that we give thanks to God and pray to Him for us in greater numbers (10.4.6). For Augustine does not respond only to the question: Why do I confess to you, God, who know all in advance? Augustine speaks of "doing the truth" (*veritatem facere*), which does not come down to revealing, unveiling, nor to informing in the order of cognitive reason. Perhaps it comes down to *testifying*. He responds to the question of public, that is to say, written testimony. A written testimony seems more public and thus, as some would be tempted to think, more in conformity with the essence of testimony, that is also to say, of its survival through the test of testamentary attestation. I want "to do the truth," he says, in my heart, in front of you, in my confession, but also "in my writing before many witnesses" (*in stilo autem meo coram multis testibus*) (10.1.1). And if he confesses in writing (*in litteris, per has litteras*) (9.12.33; 10.3.4), it is because he wants to leave a trace for his brothers to come in charity in order to stir up also, at the same time as his, the love of readers (*qui haec legunt*) (11.1.1).[2] This moment of writing is done for "afterwards" [*après*]. But it also

follows the conversion. It remains the trace of a present moment of
the confession that would have no sense without such a conversion,
without this address to the brother readers: as if the act of confession and of conversion having *already* taken place between God
and him, being as it were written (it is an *act* in the sense of archive
or memory), it was necessary to add a *post-scriptum*—the *Confessions*, nothing less—addressed to brothers, to those who are
called to recognize themselves as the sons of God and brothers
among themselves. Friendship here has to be interpreted as charity
and as fraternity. But the address to God itself already implies the
possibility and the necessity of this *post-scriptum* that is originarily
essential to it. Its irreducibility is interpreted finally, but we won't
elaborate on that here, in accord with the Augustinian thought of
revelation, memory, and time.

—Would you say that every *post-scriptum* necessarily lets itself be
interpreted in the same horizon? And that it has the same structure?

—No, not without numerous precautions. But can a *post-scriptum* ever *be interpreted*, in the sense of hermeneutic reading as well
as of musical performance, for example, without composing at least
indirectly with the Augustinian scansion or score [*partition*]? An
analogous question could be posed for all that we in the West call
autobiography, whatever the singularity of its "here and now."

—Do you mean that every "here and now" of a Western autobiography is already in memory of the *Confessions*' "here and now"?

—Yes, but the *Confessions* themselves were already, in their wild-
est present, in their date, in their place, an act of memory. Let us
leave Augustine here, although he always haunts certain landscapes
of apophatic mysticism. (Meister Eckhart cites him often; he often
cites the "without" of Saint Augustine, that quasi-negative predication of the singular without concept, for example: "God is wise
without wisdom, good *without* goodness, powerful *without* power.") In this place of retreat you invited me to, in this town of

familial exile where your mother has not finished dying, on the shore of the Mediterranean, I was able to carry with me, for these two weeks, only extracts from the *Cherubinic Wanderer* of Angelus Silesius[3] and the manuscripts of this volume here. All the time I am wondering if this work of Silesius indeed comes under negative theology. Are there sure criteria available to decide the belonging, virtual or actual, of a discourse to negative theology? Negative theology is not a genre, first of all because it is not an art, a literary art, even if, as Leibniz justly remarked of Silesius, it is a matter there also of "German poems . . . poems beautiful besides" full of "difficult metaphors." Is there, to take up again an expression of Mark Taylor's, a "classic" negative theology?[4] One can doubt this, and surely we shall have to return to this grave and limitless question. If the consequent unfolding of so many discourses (logical, onto-logical, theo-logical or not) inevitably leads to conclusions whose form or content is similar to negative theology, where are the "classic" frontiers of negative theology? The fact remains that the finale, the conclusion (*Beschluß*) of this book, and this leads us back to the question of the addressee, is an ultimate address. It says something of the end of discourse itself and is an address to the friend, the extremity of the envoi, the hail, or the farewell [*de l'envoi, du salut ou de l'adieu*]:

> Freund es ist auch genug. Jm fall du mehr wilt lesen,
> So geh und werde selbst die Schrifft und selbst das Wesen.

> Friend, let this be enough; if you wish to read beyond,
> Go and become yourself the writ and yourself the essence.
>
> (6: 263)

—The friend, who is male rather than female, is asked, recommended, enjoined, *prescribed* to render himself, by reading, beyond reading: beyond at least the legibility of what is currently readable, beyond the final signature—and for that reason to write. Not to write this or that that falls outside his writing as a note, a *nota bene* or a *post-scriptum* letting writing in its turn fall behind the written, but for the friend himself to become the written or Writing, to become the essence that writing will have treated. (No) more place, starting from there, beyond, but nothing more is told us beyond, for a *post-scriptum.* The *post-scriptum* will be the debt or the duty. It will have to, it should, be resorbed into a writing that would be nothing other than the essence that would be nothing other than the being-friend or the becoming-friend of the other. The friend will only become what he is, to wit, the friend, he will only have become the friend at the moment when he will have read that, which is to say, when he will have read beyond—to wit, when he will have gone, and one goes there, beyond, to give oneself up, only by becoming writing through writing. The becoming (*Werden*), the becoming-friend, the becoming-writing, and the essence (*Wesen*) would be the same here.

—Certainly, but this essence (*Wesen*) that, in wanting to read more, the friend would become in writing, in writing itself, in scripting itself [*en s'écrivant, en s'écriturant*], this essence will have *been* nothing before this becoming, that is, before this writing prescribed to the friend-reader. This essence is born from nothing and tends toward nothing. For earlier, didn't Silesius say . . .

—By what right are these aphorisms, these sententious fragments, or these poetic flashes linked together, as if they formed the continuous tissue of a syllogism? The final *Beschluß* is not the conclusion of a demonstration, but the farewell of an envoi. Each speaking [*parole*] is independent. In any case, you cannot logically connect them in any manner without posing this problem of logic, form, rhetoric, or poetics. You cannot treat this peregrination of writing as a treatise of philosophy or theology, not even as a sermon or a hymn.

—Certainly, but in what remains the same book, one also read:

> *Nichts werden ist GOtt werden.*
> Nichts wird was zuvor ist: wirstu nicht vor zu nicht,
> So wirstu nimmermehr gebohrn vom ewgen Licht.

To become Nothing is to become God
Nothing becomes what is before: if you do not become nothing,
Never will you be born of eternal light.

(6: 130)

How is this *becoming* to be thought? *Werden*: at once birth and change, formation and transformation. This coming to being starting from nothing and *as nothing, as God and as Nothing,* as the Nothing itself, this birth that *carries itself* without premise, this becoming-self as becoming-God—or Nothing—that is what appears impossible, more than impossible, the most impossible possible, more impossible than the impossible if the impossible is the simple negative modality of the possible.

—This thought seems strangely familiar to the experience of what is called deconstruction. Far from being a methodical technique, a possible or necessary procedure, unrolling the law of a program and applying rules, that is, unfolding possibilities, deconstruction has often been defined as the very experience of the (impossible) possibility of the impossible,[5] of the most impossible, a condition that deconstruction shares with the gift,[6] the "yes," the "come," decision, testimony, the secret, etc. And perhaps death.

—The becoming-nothing, as becoming-self or as becoming-God, the becoming (*Werden*) as the engendering *of* the other, *ever since* the other, that is what, according to Angelus Silesius, is possible, but as more impossible still than the impossible. This "more," this beyond, this *hyper* (*über*) obviously introduces an absolute heterogeneity in the order and in the modality of the possible. The possibility of the impossible, of the "more impossible" that as such is also possible ("more impossible than the impossible"), marks an absolute interruption in the regime of the possible that nonetheless remains, if this can be said, in place. When Silesius writes:

Das überunmöglichste ist möglich.
Du kanst mit deinem Pfeil die Sonne nicht erreichen,
Ich kan mit meinem wol die ewge Sonn bestreichen.

The most impossible is possible
With your arrow you cannot reach the sun,
With mine I can sweep under my fire the eternal sun.

(6: 153)

The *über* of *überunmöglichste*, moreover, can signify just as well "most" or "more than": the most impossible or the more than impossible. Elsewhere:

Geh hin, wo du nicht kanst: sih, wo du sihest nicht:
Hör wo nichts schallt und klingt, so bistu wo GOtt
spricht.

Go there where you cannot; see where you do not see;
Hear where nothing rings or sounds, so are you where
God speaks.

(1: 199)

—The possibility of the impossible, of the "most impossible," of the more impossible than the most impossible, that recalls, unless it announces, what Heidegger says of death: "die Möglichkeit der schlechthinnigen Daseinsunmöglichkeit" ("the possibility of the absolute impossibility of Dasein").[7] What is, for *Dasein*, for its possibility, purely and simply impossible is what is possible, and death is its name. I wonder if that is a matter of a purely formal analogy. What if negative theology were speaking at bottom of the mortality of *Dasein*? And of its heritage? Of what is written after it, according to [*d'après*] it? We shall no doubt come back to this.

—All the apophatic mystics can also be read as powerful discourses on death, on the (impossible) possibility of the proper death of being-there that speaks, and that speaks of what carries away, interrupts, denies, or annihilates its speaking as well as its own *Dasein*. Between the existential analytic of being-to-death or being-for-death, in *Being and Time*, and the remarks of Heidegger on the theological, the theiological, and above all on a theology in which the word "being"[8] would not even appear, the coherence seems to me profound and the continuity rigorous.

—What would this hyper-impossibility have to do, in the singular obscurity of this sun, with friendship? With the address to the friend?

—The questions of address and destination, of love and friendship (beyond even determinations of *philia* or charity) could lead us in numerous directions. In our place here and in the little time at our disposal this summer, allow me to privilege one, only one, of these questions. What reunites us here, the two of us, after the Calgary colloquium on negative theology? Mark Taylor often questioned himself on the experience of what gathers or reunites, of *gathering*.[9] This colloquium has already taken place. We were not there. A colloquium is a place one goes to (as to a synagogue, that place one comes to to gather together) to address oneself to others. At this colloquium in which we were not able, despite our desire, to participate directly, we had nonetheless promised, you recall, to bring ourselves together in a certain form, with some delay, and by writing: that is, *after the event* [après coup]. In any case, the possibility of a colloquium—and then of speaking with one another—was indeed announced to *us*, a colloquium whose title bore the words "negative theology." This project could be announced only under certain conditions. What was required was to desire to share there. What was one already able to share there? Who then addresses whom? And what does "friendship" signify in this case?

—From the very beginning, and from the first word of our promise, you remember, we had thought we had to forgo, for countless reasons, a *post-scriptum* that was a long and detailed response. We have had above all to forgo an original discussion that is on the same scale as so many contributions whose richness and rigor, diversity too, we have admired and that we will still have much to learn from and to meditate on. Every immediate response would be hasty and presumptuous, in truth irresponsible and not very "*responsive.*" It will be necessary to *postpone* once more a true *post-scriptum.*

—What you seemed to care about, you said to me, was to testify to a gratitude whose meaning would not be without relation to what is called here negative theology and that in its turn would not risk, *not too much*, becoming ingratitude, an inversion that lies in wait to threaten all apophatic movements. And then no doubt you have more affinity at the outset, an immediate affinity, given or cultivated, with particular participants, with particular discourses held here . . .

—What's the use of denying it? But also what's the use of remarking or underlining it? These shared portions [*partages*], these common inclinations, or these crossed paths appear from the reading of our respective texts, in particular those that are published right here. And if I have not yet ever met the other participants of the colloquium, it is also true that my friendship and my admiration, my gratefulness to Mark Taylor, are not separable from his thought or his writings—including the text which he is publishing in the proceedings of this colloquium.

Nevertheless, I would like to speak of another "community" (a word I never much liked, because of its connotation of participation, indeed fusion, identification: I see in it as many threats as promises), of another being-together than this one here, of another gathering-together of singularities, of another friendship, even though that friendship no doubt owes the essential to being- or gathering-together. I mean the friendship that permits such a meeting, and that very polylogue through which are written and read those for whom "negative theology," through the enigma of its name and its original lack of meaning, still signifies something and pushes them to address one another *under this name, in this name, and by this title.*

How, today, can one speak—that is, speak together, address someone, testify—on the subject of and in the name of negative theology?

How can that take place today, today still, so long after the inaugural openings of the *via negativa*? Is negative theology a "topic" [English in original—Ed.]? How would what still comes to us under the domestic, European, Greek, and Christian term of negative theology, of negative way, of apophatic discourse, be the chance of an incomparable translatability in principle without limit? Not of a universal tongue, of an ecumenism or of some consensus, but of a tongue to come that can be shared more than ever? One should wonder what signifies in this regard the friendship of the friend, if one withdraws it, like negative theology itself, from all its dominant determinations in the Greek or Christian world,[10] from the fraternal (fraternalist) and phallocentric schema of *philia* or charity, as well as from a certain arrested form of democracy.

—Friendship and translation, then, and the experience of translation as friendship, that is what you seem to wish we were speaking about. It is true that one imagines with difficulty a translation, in the current sense of the term, whether it is competent or not, without some *philein*, without some love or friendship, without some "lovence" [*aimance*], as you would say, borne [*portée*] toward the thing, the text, or the other to be translated. Even if hatred can sharpen the vigilance of a translator and motivate a demystifying interpretation, this hatred still reveals an intense form of desire, interest, indeed fascination.

—Those are experiences of translation, it seems to me, that make up this "Colloquium," and almost all the authors even give this to be remarked. Let it be said in passing, a translation (the nonoriginal version of a textual event that will have preceded it) also shares that curious status of the *post-scriptum* about which we are going around in circles.

—In which, rather, we discuss [*nous débattons*], we flounder [*nous nous débattons*]. How does negative theology always run the risk of resembling an exercise of translation? An exercise and nothing but? And an exercise in the form of a *post-scriptum*? How would this risk also give it a chance?

—Let's start again from this proposition, if you like: "What is called 'negative theology,' in an idiom of Greco-Latin filiation, is a language [*langage*]."

—Only a language? More or less than a language? Isn't it also what questions and casts suspicion on the very essence or possibility of language? Isn't it what, in essence, exceeds language, so that the "essence" of negative theology would carry itself outside of language?

—Doubtless, but what is called "negative theology," in an idiom of Greco-Latin filiation, is a language, at least, that says, in one mode or another, what we have just specified about language, that is, about itself. How does one leap out of this circle?

—Consequently, to believe you, an admissible *disputing* [contestation *recevable*] of this proposition of the type S is P ("what is called 'NT' . . . is a language," etc.) could not take the form of a refutation. It could not consist in giving a critique of its falseness, but in suspecting its vagueness, emptiness, or obscurity, in accusing it of not being able to determine either the subject or the attribute of that judgment, of not even proving this learned ignorance, in the sense ennobled by Nicolas of Cusa or certain supporters of negative theology. The proposition ("What is called 'negative theology' . . . is a language") has no rigorously determinable reference: neither in its subject nor in its attribute, we just said, but not even in its copula. For it happens that, however little is known of the said negative theology . . .

—You avow then that we do indeed know something about it, we don't speak of it in the void, we come *after* this knowledge, however minimal and precarious. We preunderstand it . . .

—The preunderstanding then would be the fact from which we should indeed start, in relation to which we would be placed-after [*post-posés*]. We come *after the fact* [après le fait]: and the discursive possibilities of the *via negativa* are doubtless exhausted, that is what remains for us to think. Besides, they will be very quickly exhausted; they will always consist in an intimate and immediate exhaustion [*exhaustion*] of themselves, as if they could not have any history. That is why the slightness of the reference corpus (here *The Cherubinic Wanderer*, for example) or the rarefaction of examples should not be a serious problem. We are in absolute exemplarity as in the aridity of the desert, for the essential tendency is to formalizing rarefaction. Impoverishment is de rigueur.

—These discursive possibilities are exhausted as formal possibilities, no doubt, and if we formalize to the extreme the procedures of this theology. Which seems feasible and tempting. Then nothing remains for you, not even a name or a reference. You can speak of exhaustion [*d'épuisement*] only in the perspective of this complete formalization and in posing as extrinsic to this formal or conceptual completeness those "difficult metaphors . . . inclining almost to Godlessness," that poetic beauty, too, which Leibniz speaks about concerning Angelus Silesius. Thus you would oppose one form to the other, that of onto-logical formalism to that of poetics, and would remain prisoner of a problematic opposition between form and content. But this so traditional disjunction between concept and metaphor, between logic, rhetoric, and poetics, between sense and language, isn't it a philosophical prejudgment not only that one can or must deconstruct, but that, in its very possibility, the event named "negative theology" will have powerfully contributed to calling into question?

—I only wanted to recall that we preunderstood *already* and therefore that we write *after* preunderstanding negative theology as a "critique" (for the moment let's not say a "deconstruction") of the proposition, of the verb "be" in the third person indicative and of everything that, in the determination of the essence, depends on this mood, this time, and this person: briefly, a critique of ontology, of theology, and of language. To say "What is called 'negative theology', in an idiom of Greco-Latin filiation, is a language" is then to say little, almost nothing, perhaps less than nothing.

—Negative theology means (to say) very little, almost nothing, perhaps something other than something. Whence its inexhaustible exhaustion . . .

—That being the case, can one be authorized to speak of this apparently elementary *factum*, perhaps indeterminate, obscure, or void and yet hardly contestable, to wit, our preunderstanding of what is "called 'negative theology' . . . ," etc.? What we are identifying under these two words, today, isn't it first of all a corpus, at once open and closed, given, well-ordered, a set of statements [*un ensemble d'énoncés*] recognizable either by their family resemblance [English parenthetical gloss in the original—Ed.] or because they come under a regular logicodiscursive type whose recurrence lends itself to a formalization? This formalization can become mechanical . . .

—All the more mechanizable and easily reproducible, falsifiable, exposed to forgery and counterfeit since the statement of negative theology empties itself by definition, by vocation, of all intuitive plentitude. *Kenōsis* of discourse. If a phenomenological type of rule is followed for distinguishing between a full intuition and an empty or symbolic intending [*visée*] forgetful of the originary perception supporting it, then the apophatic statements *are, must be* on the side of the empty and then of mechanical, indeed purely verbal, repetition of phrases without actual or full intentional meaning. Apophatic statements represent what Husserl identifies as the moment of *crisis* (forgetting of the full and originary intuition, empty functioning of symbolic language, objectivism, etc.). But in revealing the originary and final necessity of this crisis, in denouncing from the language of crisis the snares of intuitive consciousness and of phenomenology, they destabilize the very axiomatics of the phenomenological, which is also the ontological and transcendental, critique. Emptiness is essential and necessary to them. If they guard against this, it is through the moment of prayer or the hymn. But this protective moment remains structurally exterior to the purely apophatic instance, that is, to *negative* theology as such, if there is any in the strict sense, which can at times be doubted. The value, the *evaluation*, of the quality, of the intensity, or of the force of events of negative theology would then result from this *relation* that articulates *this* void [*vide*] on the plentitude of a prayer or an attribution (theo-logical, theio-logical, or onto-logical) negated [*niée*], let's say denegated [*déniée*]. The criterion is the measure of a *relation*, and this relation is stretched between two poles, one of which must be that of positivity de-negated.

—From what does this redoubtable mechanicity result, the facility that there can be in imitating or fabricating negative theology (or, as well, a poetry of the same inspiration, of which we indeed have examples)? From the fact, I believe, that the very functioning of these statements resides in a formalization. This formalization essentially does without, tends essentially to do without all content and every idiomatic signifier, every presentation or representation, images and even names of God, for example, in this tongue or that culture. In brief, negative theology lets itself be approached (preunderstood) as a corpus largely archived with propositions whose logical modalities, grammar, lexicon, and very semantics are already accessible to us, at least for what is determinable in them.

—Whence the possibility of a canonizing monumentalization of works that, obeying laws, seem docile to the norms of a genre and an art. These works repeat traditions; they present themselves as iterable, influential or influenceable, objects of transfer, of credit and of discipline. For there are masters and disciples there. Recall Dionysius and Timothy. There are exercises and formations, there are schools, in the Christian mystical tradition as well as in an ontotheological or meontological (more Greek) tradition, in its exoteric or esoteric forms.

—Certainly, and he is already a disciple, however inspired, the one who wrote that not only God but the deity surpasses knowledge, that the singularity of the unknown God overflows the essence and the divinity, thwarting in this manner the oppositions of the negative and the positive, of being and nothingness, of thing and nonthing—thus transcending all the theological attributes:

> *Der unerkandte GOtt.*
> Was GOtt ist weiß man nicht: Er ist nicht Licht, nicht Geist,
> Nicht Wonnigkeit, nicht Eins [Derrida's version: Nicht
>   Wahrheit, Einheit, Eins], nicht was man Gottheit heist:
> Nicht Weißheit, nicht Verstand, nicht Liebe, Wille, Gütte:
> Kein Ding, kein Unding auch, kein Wesen, kein Gemütte:
> Er ist was ich, und du, und keine Creatur,
> Eh wir geworden sind was Er ist, nie erfuhr.

> *The unknowable God*
> What God is one knows not: He is not light, not spirit,
> Not delight, not one [Not truth, unity, one], not what is
>   called divinity:
> Not wisdom, not intellect, not love, will, goodness:
> No thing, no no-thing either, no essence, no concern:
> He is what I, or you, or any other creature,
> Before we became what He is, have never come to know.
>   (4: 21)

—The following maxim [*sentence*] is precisely addressed to Saint Augustine as if to someone close, a master and a predecessor that he can amicably or respectfully challenge: "Stop, my *Augustine*: before you have penetrated God to the bottom [*ergründen*], one will find the entire sea in a small pit [*Grüblein*]" (4: 22).

—Angelus Silesius had his own peculiar genius, but already he was repeating, continuing, importing, transporting. He would transfer or translate in all the senses of this term because he already *was post-writing*. This heir kept the archive, kept in memory the teaching of Christoph Köler. He had read Tauler, Ruysbroeck, Boehme, and above all Eckhart.

—What we ought to start from, if I understand you rightly (and this would be the *a priori* of our *a posteriori*, to wit, of this *post-scriptum* we are engaged in), is this astonishing *fact* [fait], this *already done* [déjà fait], this *all done* [tout fait]: while negating or effacing all, while proceeding to eradicate every predicate and claiming to inhabit the desert . . .

—The desert is one of the beautiful and difficult metaphors that Leibniz was no doubt speaking of, but I am also struck by its recurrence, in other words, by the *typical striking* that reproduces the metaphor like a seal. Thus:

> *Man muß noch über GOtt.*
> . . . Wol sol ich dann nun hin?
> Jch muß noch über GOtt in eine wüste ziehn.
>
> *One must go beyond God*
> . . . What should my quest then be?
> I must beyond God into a desert flee.
>
> (1: 7)

Or again:

> *Die Einsamkeit.*
> Die Einsamket ist noth: doch sey nur nicht gemein:
> So kanstu überall in einer Wüsten seyn.
>
> *Solitude*
> Solitude is necessary, but be only not (in) public,
> So you can everywhere be in a desert.
>
> (2: 117)

And elsewhere it is a question of "desert times" (*in diser wüsten Zeit* [3: 184]). Isn't the desert a paradoxical figure of the *aporia*? No [*pas de*] marked out [*tracé*] or assured passage, no route in any case, at the very most trails that are not reliable ways, the paths are not yet cleared [*frayés*], unless the sand has already re-covered them. But isn't the uncleared way also the condition of *decision* or *event*, which consists in opening the way, in *(sur)passing*, thus in going *beyond*? In (sur)passing the aporia?

—Despite this desert, then, what we call negative theology grows and cultivates itself as a memory, an institution, a history, a discipline. It is a culture, with its archives and its tradition. It accumulates the *acts* of a tongue [*langue*]. That in particular is what the phrase "What is called 'negative theology,' in an idiom of Greco-Latin filiation, is a language" would suggest. However much one recalls (one precisely must recall and recall that that proves the possibility of the memory kept) that negative theology "consists," through its claim to depart from all consistency, in a language that does not cease testing the very limits of language, and exemplarily those of propositional, theoretical, or constative language . . .

—By that, negative theology would be not only a language and a testing of language, but above all the most thinking, the most exacting, the most intractable experience of the "essence" of language: a discourse on language, a "monologue" (in the heterological sense that Novalis or Heidegger gives to this word) in which language and tongue speak for themselves and record [*prennent acte de*] that *die Sprache spricht.* Whence this poetic or fictional dimension, at times ironic, always allegorical, about which some would say that it is only a form, an appearance, or a simulacrum. . . . It is true that, simultaneously, this arid fictionality tends to denounce images, figures, idols, rhetoric. An iconoclastic fiction must be thought.

—However much one says, then, that beyond the theorem and constative description, the discourse of negative theology "consists" in exceeding essence and language, by testifying it *remains.*

—What does "remain" mean here? Is it a modality of "being"?

—I don't know. Perhaps this, precisely, that this theology would be nothing . . .

—To be nothing, wouldn't that be its secret or declared vow? What do you believe you are thus threatening it with? Our discussion still supposes that this theology is something (determinable) and not nothing and wants to be or become something rather than nothing. Now we meant, just a moment ago too, to claim the contrary . . .

—A question of reading or hearing [*l'oreille*]. In any case, negative theology would be nothing, very simply nothing, if this excess or this surplus (with regard to language) did not imprint some mark on some singular events of language and did not leave some remains on the body of a tongue . . .

—A corpus, in sum.

—Some trace remains right in this corpus, becomes this corpus as *sur-vivance* of apophasis (more than life and more than death), survivance of an internal onto-logico-semantic auto-destruction: there will have been absolute rarefaction, the desert will have taken place, nothing will have taken place but this place. Certainly, the "unknowable God" ("*Der unerkandte GOtt*," 4: 21), the ignored or unrecognized God that we spoke about says nothing: of him there is nothing said that might hold . . .

—Save his name [*Sauf son nom*; "Safe, his name"] . . .

—Save the name that names nothing that might hold, not even a divinity (*Gottheit*), nothing whose withdrawal [*dérobement*] does not carry away every phrase that tries to measure itself against him. "God" "is" the name of this bottomless collapse, of this endless desertification of language. But the trace of this negative operation is inscribed *in* and *on* and *as* the *event* (what *comes*, what there is and which is always singular, what finds in this kenōsis the most decisive condition of its coming or its upsurging). *There is* this event, which remains, even if this remnance is not more substantial, more essential than this God, more ontologically determinable than this name of God of whom it is said that he names nothing that is, neither this nor that. It is even said of him that he is not what is *given there* in the sense of *es gibt*: He is not what gives, his is beyond all gifts ("*GOtt über alle Gaben*," 4: 30).

—Don't forget that that is said in the course of a prayer. What is prayer? No, one should not ask "What is prayer?," prayer in general. It is necessary to attempt to think prayer, in truth to test it out (to pray *it*, if one can say that, and transitively) through this particular prayer, this singular prayer in which or toward which prayer in general *strains itself*. For this particular prayer asks nothing, all the while asking more than everything. It asks God to give himself rather than gifts: "Giebstu mir dich nicht selbst, so hastu nichts gegeben"; "If you don't give yourself to me, then you have given nothing." Which interprets again the divinity of God as gift or desire of giving. And prayer is this interpretation, the very body of this interpretation. *In* and *on*, you said, that implies, apparently, some *topos* . . .

— . . . or some *khōra* (body without body, absent body but unique body and place [*lieu*] of everything, in the place of everything, interval, place [*place*], spacing). Would you also say of *khōra*, as you were just doing in a murmur, "save its name" [*sauf son nom*; safe, its name]? Everything secret is played out here. For this location displaces and disorganizes all our onto-topological prejudices, in particular the objective science of space. *Khōra* is over there but more "here" than any "here" . . .

—You well know that, in nearly all its Greek, Christian, or Jewish networks [*filières*], the *via negativa* conjugates reference to

God, the name of God, with the experience of place. The desert is also a figure of the pure place. But figuration in general results from this spatiality, from this locality of the word [*parole*].

—Yes, Angelus Silesius writes this about the word (*das Wort*), that is to say, about the divine word as well, and some translate *Wort* here just simply by God:

> *Der Ort ist dass Wort.*
> Der ort und's *Wort* ist Eins, und wäre nicht der
>   ort
> (Bey Ewger Ewigkeit!) es wäre nicht das *Wort.*
>
> *The place is the word*
> The place and the *word* is one, and were the place not
> (of all eternal eternity!) the *word* would not be.
>
> (1: 205)

—Not objective nor earthly, this place comes under no geography, geometry, or geophysics. It is not *that in which* is found a subject or an object. It is found in us, whence the equivocal necessity of at once recognizing it and getting rid of it:

> *Der Orth is selbst in dir.*
> Nicht du bist in dem Orth, der Orth der ist in dir!
> Wirfstu jhn auß, so steht die Ewigkeit schon hier.
>
> *The place is itself in you*
> It is not you in the place, the place is in you!
> Cast it out, and here is already eternity.
>
> (1: 185)

—The here (*hier*) of eternity is situated there, already (*schon*): already there, it situates this throwing [*jet*] or this throwing up [*rejet*] (*Auswerfen* is difficult to translate: at once exclusion, putting aside, throwing out [*rejet*], but first of all throwing that puts outside, that produces the outside and thus *space*, separates the place from itself: *khōra*). It is from this already that the *post-scriptum* finds its place—and fatally.

—As if in response, it is already in correspondence with what Mark Taylor will have written of the "pretext of the text," which "is a before that is (always) yet to come." Or again when he plays without playing with the word, the word for word, such as it takes place or takes up residence in the other's tongue: "What is the *Ort* of the *W-ort?*"[11]

—The event remains at once *in* and *on* language, then, within and at the surface (a surface open, exposed, immediately over-flowed, outside of itself). The event remains in and on the mouth, on the tip [*bout*] of the tongue, as is said in English and French, or on the edge of the lips passed over by words that *carry* themselves toward God. They are *carried* [*portés*], both *exported* and *deported*, by a movement of *ference* (transference, reference, difference) to-ward God. They name God, speak of him, speak *him*, speak *to him*, *let him speak in them*, let themselves be carried by him, make (themselves) a reference to just what the name supposes to name beyond itself, the nameable beyond the name, the unnameable nameable. As if it was necessary both to save the name and to save everything except the name, *save the name* [sauf le nom], as if it was necessary to lose the name in order to save what bears the name, or that toward which one goes through the name. But to lose the name is not to attack it, to destroy it or wound it. On the contrary, to lose the name is quite simply to respect it: as name. That is to say, to pronounce it, which comes down to traversing it toward the other, the other whom it names and who bears it. To pronounce it without pronouncing it. To forget it by calling it, by recalling it (to oneself), which comes down to calling or recalling the other . . .

—Certainly, but it is then necessary to stop submitting language, and the name in language (by the way, is the name, the proper name or the name par excellence *in* language and what would this inclusion mean?) to generality, to whatever figure or topological schema? We speak here *in* and *on* a language that, while being opened by this *ference*, says the inadequation of the reference, the insufficiency or the lapse of knowing, its incompetence as to what it is said to be the knowing of. Such an inadequation translates and betrays the absence of a common measure between the opening, openness [*apérité*], revelation, knowledge on the one hand and on the other a certain absolute secret, nonprovisional, heterogeneous to all manifestation. This secret is not a reserve of potential [*potentiel*] knowing, a potential [*en puissance*] manifestation. And the language of ab-negation or of renunciation is not negative: not only because it does not state in the mode of descriptive predication and of the indicative proposition simply affected with a negation ("this is not that"), but because it denounces as much as it renounces; and it denounces, enjoining; it prescribes overflowing this insufficiency; it mandates, *it necessitates* doing the impossible, necessitates going (*Geh*, Go!) there where one cannot go. Passion of, for, the place, again. I shall say in French: *il y a lieu de* (which means *il faut*, "it is necessary," "there is ground for") rendering oneself *there where* it is impossible to go. Over there, toward the name, toward the beyond of the name *in* the name. Toward what, toward he or she who remains—save the name [*sauf le nom*, or "safe, the name"— Ed.]. Going where it is possible to go would not be a displacement or a decision, it would be the irresponsible unfolding of a program. The sole decision possible passes through the madness of the undecidable and the impossible: to go where (*wo*, *Ort*, *Wort*) it is impossible to go. Recall:

> Geh hin, wo du nicht kanst: sih, wo du sihest nicht:
> Hör wo nichts schallt und klingt, so bistu wo Gott spricht.
>
> (1: 199)

—According to you, it is this normative denunciation on the ground of impossibility, this sweet rage against language, this jealous anger of language within itself and against itself, it is this passion that leaves the mark of a scar in that place where the

impossible takes place, isn't it? Over there, on the other side of the
world? The other side *of the* world, is that still the world, in the
world, the other world or the other *of the* world, everything save the
world [*tout sauf le monde*, also "totally safe, the world"—Ed.]?

—Yes, the wound is there, over there. Is there some other thing,
ever, that may be legible? Some other thing than the trace of a
wound? And some other thing that may ever take place? Do you
know another definition of event?

—But nothing is more illegible than a wound, as well. I suppose
that in your eyes legibility and illegibility do not equal two in this
place. According to you, it is this trace in any case that becomes
legible, renders and renders itself legible: in and on language, that
is, at the edge of language . . .

—There is only the edge in language . . . That is, reference. From
the supposed fact that there is never anything but reference, an
irreducible reference, one can *just as well* conclude that the referent—everything save the name [*tout sauf le nom*, also "totally safe,
the name"—Ed.]—is or is not indispensable. All history of negative
theology, I bet, plays itself out in this brief and slight axiom.

—"At the edge of language" would then mean: "at the edge as
language," in the same and double movement: withdrawing [*dérobement*] and overflowing [*débordement*]. But as the moment and
the force, as the *movements* of the injunction take place *over the edge*
[par-dessus bord], as they draw their energy *from having already
taken place*—even if it is as a promise—the legible-illegible text, the
theologico-negative maxim [*sentence*] remains as a *post-scriptum*. It
is originarily a *post-scriptum*, it comes after the event . . .

—an event, if I understand right, that would have the form of a
seal, as if, witness without witness, it were committed to keeping a
secret, the event sealed with an indecipherable signature, a set of
initials, a line [*dessin*] before the letter.

—The sealed event corresponding to the experience of a *trait* (drawn line, *Zug*, edge, border, overflowing, relation to the other, *Zug*, *Bezug*, ference, reference to some *other* thing than self, differance), the deferred action [*l'après-coup*] is indeed the coming of a writing after the other: *post-scriptum.*

—The trace of this wounded writing that bears the stigmata of its own proper inadequation: signed, assumed, claimed . . .

— . . . of its own proper disproportion also, of its *hubris* thus countersigned: that cannot be a simple mark identical to self . . .

— . . . as if there ever were any . . .

—That cannot be a signature uneffaced, ineffaceable, invulnerable, legible for what it is on a surface, right on a support that would only equal one with (it)self. The very surface serving as support for the signature [*le subjectile même*] remains improbable. This mark takes place after taking place, in a slight, discreet, but powerful movement of dis-location, on the unstable and divided edge of what is called language. The very unity of what is called language becomes enigmatic and uncertain there.

And so the phrase "What is called 'negative theology' . . . is a language" says at once too much and too little. It no longer has the intelligibility of a sure axiom, no longer gives the chance of a consensus, the charter of a colloquium, or the assured space of a communication.

—Let's not yet discredit the phrase. Let's provisionally keep it, as a guiding thread, as if we had need of it and the desire of going further.

—Don't all the apophatic theologemes have the status or rather the movement, the instability of this trajectory? Don't they resemble arrows, darts [*traits*], a grouped firing of arrows destined to point in the same direction? But an arrow is only an arrow; it is never an end in itself. It is everything save what it aims for, save what it strikes, even, indeed, save what it wounds; this is what makes the arrow miss even that which it touches, which thereby remains safe . . .

—Silesius says this well when he speaks precisely of the possibility of the most impossible or of the more than the most impossible ("Das überunmöglichste ist möglich"). It specifies, you recall:

> With your arrow you cannot reach the sun,
> With mine I can sweep under my fire the eternal sun.
>
> (6: 153)

—Let's keep this proposition ("What is called 'negative theology' . . . is a language"). Let's try to question it in its most manifest meaning, *at face value* [in English in original—Ed.]. And let's come back to the theme of *philein*, let's say rather of lovence [*aimance*] as transfer or translation.

—These themes are not localizable, but let's go on.

—Do you want us to act as if they were? The appearance gives us to believe that the expression "negative theology" has no *strict* equivalent outside two traditions, philosophy or ontotheology of Greek provenance, New Testament theology or Christian mysticism. These two trajectories, these two paths [*trajets*] thus arrowed would cross each other in the heart of what we call negative theology. Such a crossing . . .

—Everything here, you realize, seems *crucial*: the crossroads of these two paths, the *kreuzweise Durchstreichung* under which Heidegger erases the word being (which his theology to come would have had, he says, to dispense with), and the *Gevier* to which he claims then to refer, the Christian cross under which Marion himself erases the word "God" (a way, perhaps, to save the name of God, to shield it from all onto-theological idolatry: God without

Being [*Dieu sans l'être*, also understandable as "God without being God" and hearable as "God without letter"; also the title of a book by Jean-Luc Marion that has been translated as *God Without Being: Hors Texte*, by Thomas A. Carlson (Chicago: University of Chicago Press, 1991)—Ed.].

—That's true. In any case, the expression "negative theology" names most often a discursive experience that is situated at one of the angles formed by the crossing of these two lines. Even if one line is then always *crossed* [English parenthetical gloss in the original—Ed.], this line is situated in that place. Whatever the translations, analogies, transpositions, transferences, metaphors, never has any discourse expressly given itself this title (negative theology, apophatic method, *via negativa*) in the thoughts of Jewish, Muslim, Buddhist culture.

—Are you sure that this title has never been claimed by any author for his very own discourse, even in the traditions you invoke?

—I was only wanting to suggest that in the cultural or historical zone in which the expression "negative theology" appears as a sort of domestic and controlled appellation, the zone in sum of that Christian philosophy whose concept Heidegger was saying was as mad and contradictory as that of a squared circle, apophasis has always represented a sort of paradoxical hyperbole.

—That's a name quite philosophical and quite Greek.

—From this paradoxical hyperbole, let's retain here the trait necessary to a brief demonstration. Let's be more modest, to a working hypothesis. Here it is. What permits localizing negative theology in a historial site and identifying its very own idiom is also what uproots it from its rooting. What assigns it a proper place is what expropriates it and *engages* it thus in a movement of universalizing translation. In other words, it is what engages it in the element of the most shareable [*partageable*] discourse, for example,

that of this conversation or of this colloquium in which are crossed
thematics Christian and non-Christian (Jewish, Muslim, Hindu,
Buddhist, etc.), philosophical and nonphilosophical, European
and non-European, etc.

—Do you see in this *engagement* something that is allied with this
singular friendship you spoke about just a moment ago with
gratefulness—and apropos gratitude?

—I don't know. All this remains very preliminary, as precipitated
as a *post-scriptum* can be. If I use words as philosophical and Greek
as "paradoxical hyperbole," I do so first of all, among other things,
to point [*faire signe*] toward a well-known passage of Plato's *Republic. Huperbolē* names the movement of transcendence that carries or transports beyond being or beingness [*étantité*] *epekeina tēs
ousias.* This excessive movement, the firing of this displacing arrow
[*cette flèche en déplacement*] encourages saying: X "is" beyond what
is, beyond being or beingness. Let X here be the Good, it matters
little for the moment, since we are analyzing the formal possibility
of saying: X "is" beyond what "is," X is without being (X) [*sans
(l')être*]. This hyperbole *announces.* It announces in a double sense:
it *signals* an open possibility, but it also *provokes* thereby the opening of the possibility. Its event is at once revealing and producing,
post-scriptum and prolegomenon, inaugural writing. Its event announces what comes and makes come what will come from now on
in all the movements in *hyper, ultra, au-delà, beyond, über,* which
will precipitate discourse or, first of all, existence. This precipita-
tion is their passion.

—You said "existence," if I understand right, in order not to say
"subject," "soul," "spirit," "ego," nor even *Da-sein.* And yet *Dasein*
is open to being as being by the possibility of going beyond the
present of what is. Passion: transcendence.

—To be sure, and Heidegger does indeed understand *Dasein*
thus: he describes the movement of its transcendence by explicitly

citing the Platonic *epekeina tēs ousias.* But then he seems to under-stand/hear the beyond as the beyond of the totality of beings and not as the beyond of being itself, in the sense of negative theology. Now the hyperbolic movements in the Platonic, Plotinian, or Neoplatonic style will not only precipitate beyond being or God insofar as he is (the supreme being [*étant*]), but beyond God even as name, as naming, named, or nameable, insofar as reference is made there to some thing. The name itself seems sometimes to be there no longer safe . . . The name itself seems sometimes to be no longer there, save [*sauf,* safe] . . .

— . . . besides, the beyond as beyond God is not a place, but a movement of transcendence that surpasses God himself, being, essence, the proper or the self-same, the *Selbst* or *Self* of God, the divinity of God (*GOttheit*)—in which it surpasses positive *theology* as well as what Heidegger proposes to call *theiology,* that is, dis-course on the divinity (*theion*) of the divine. Angelus Silesius, again, who was saying, you recall:

> *Man muß noch über GOtt.*
> . . .
> Jch muß noch über GOtt in eine wüste ziehn.
> (1: 7)

but also:

> *Die über-GOttheit.*
> Was man von GOtt gesagt, das gnüget mir noch nicht:
> Die über-GOttheit ist mein Leben und mein Liecht.
>
> *The beyond divinity*
> What was said of God, not yet suffices me:
> The beyond divinity is my life and my light.
> (1: 15)

—Carrying itself beyond, this movement radically dissociates being and knowing, and existence and knowledge. It is, as it were, a

fracture of the *cogito* (Augustinian or Cartesian) as the *cogito* gives
me to know not only *that*, but *what and who* I am. This fracture is
as valid for me as for God; it extends its crack into the analogy
between God and me, creator and creature. This time the analogy
does not repair, nor reconcile, but aggravates the dissociation.

> *Man weiß nicht was man ist.*
> Jch weiß nicht was ich bin. Jch bin nicht was ich weiß:
> Ein ding und nit ein ding: Ein stüpffchin und ein kreiß.

> *One knows not what one is*
> I know not what I am. I am not what I know:
> A thing and not a thing: a point and a circle.
>
> (1: 5)

And here is, hardly much farther, the analogy, the *wie*:

> *Jch bin wie Gott, un Gott wie ich.*
> Jch bin so groß als GOtt: Er ist als ich so klein:
> Er kan nich über mich, ich unter Jhm nicht seyn.

> *I am as God, and God as I*
> I am as big as God: He is as small as I:
> He cannot be over me, I cannot be under him.
>
> (1: 10)

—I am always sensitive to this unusual alliance of *two powers* and
of *two voices* in these poetic aphorisms or in these declarations
without appeal, above all when the *I* advances there in this way, at
once alone with God and as the example that authorizes itself to
speak for each one, to dare testify for the other (to testify for the
witness), without waiting for any response or fearing discussion.
Contrary to what we said at the beginning of our conversation,
there is also a monologism or soliloquy in these imperturbable
discourses: nothing seems to disquiet them. These two powers are,
on the one hand, that of a radical critique, of a hyper-critique after
which nothing more seems assured, neither philosophy nor theology, nor science, nor good sense, nor the least *doxa*, and *on the other*

hand, conversely, as we are settled beyond all discussion, the authority of that sententious voice that produces or reproduces mechanically its verdicts with the tone of the most dogmatic assurance: nothing or no one can oppose this, since we are in passion: the assumed contradiction and the claimed paradox.

—The double power of these two voices is not without relation to the *double bind* of ex-appropriation or of the uprooting rooting I spoke about just before. In effect, this theology launches or carries negativity as the principle of auto-destruction in the heart of each thesis; in any event, this theology suspends every thesis, all belief, all *doxa* . . .

—In which its *epokhē* has some affinity with the *skepsis* of scepticism as well as with the phenomenological reduction. And contrary to what we were saying a while ago, transcendental phenomenology, insofar as it passes through the suspension of all *doxa*, of every positing of existence, of every thesis, inhabits the same element as negative theology. One would be a good propaedeutic for the other.

—If you like, but this is not incompatible with what we said about the language of crisis. But let's leave that. *On the one hand*, then, placing the thesis in parenthesis or in quotation marks ruins each ontological or theological proposition, in truth, each philosopheme as such. In this sense, the principle of negative theology, in a movement of internal rebellion, radically contests the tradition from which it seems to come. Principle against principle. Parricide and uprooting, rupture of belonging, interruption of a sort of social contract, the one that gives right to the State, the nation, more generally to the philosophical community as rational and logocentric community. Negative theology uproots itself from there after the fact [*après coup*], in the torsion or conversion of a second movement of uprooting, as if a signature was not countersigned but contradicted in a codicil or in the remorse of a *post-scriptum* at the bottom of the contract. This contract rupture programs a whole series of analogous and recurrent movements, a whole outbidding of the *nec plus ultra* that calls to witness the *epekeina tēs ousias*, and at times without presenting itself as negative theology (Plotinus, Heidegger, Levinas).

But *on the other hand*, and in that very way, nothing is more faithful than this hyperbole to the originary ontotheological injunction. The *post-scriptum* remains a *countersignature*, even if it denies this. And, as in every human or divine signature, there the name is necessary [*il y faut le nom*]. Unless, as was suggested a moment ago, the name be what effaces itself in front of what it names. Then "the name is necessary" would mean that the name is lacking [*fait défaut*]: it must be lacking, a name is necessary [*il faut un nom*] that is lacking [*fasse défaut*]. Thus *managing to efface itself*, it *itself will be safe, will be, save itself* [sera sauf lui-même]. In the most apophatic moment, when one says: "God is not," "God is neither this nor that, neither that nor its contrary" or "being is not," etc., even then it is still a matter of saying the entity [*étant*] such as it is, in its truth, even were it meta-metaphysical, meta-ontological. It is a matter of holding the promise of saying the truth at any price, of testifying, of rendering oneself to the truth of the name, to the thing itself such as it must be named by the name, *that is, beyond the name*. The thing, save the name. It is a matter of recording the referential transcendence of which the negative way is only one way, one methodic approach, one series of stages. A prayer, too, and a testimony of love, but an "I love you" on the way to prayer and to love, always on the way. Angelus Silesius, among others, specifies this well when he adds, in a sort of note or *post-scriptum* to sentence 1: 7, "*Man muß noch über GOtt*": "beyond all one knows of God or can think of him, according to negative contemplation [*nach der verneinenden beschawung*], about which search through the *mystics*."

—Then you wouldn't say that the *Cherubinic Wanderer* comes under negative theology.

—No, certainly not in any sure, pure, and integral fashion, although the *Cherubinic Wanderer* owes much to it. But I would no more say that of any text. Conversely, I trust no text that is not in some way contaminated with negative theology, and even among those texts that apparently do not have, want, or believe they have any relation with theology in general. Negative theology is everywhere, but it is never by itself. In that way it also belongs, without fulfilling, to the space of the philosophical or onto-theological promise that it seems to break [*renier*]: to record, as we said a moment ago, the referential transcendence of language: to say God such as he is, beyond [*par delà*] his images, beyond this idol that being can still be, beyond what is said, seen, or known of him; to respond to the true name of God, to the name to which God responds and corresponds beyond the name that we know him by or hear. It is to this end that the negative procedure refuses, denies, rejects all the inadequate attributions. It does so in the name of a way of truth and in order to hear the name of a just voice. The authority of which we spoke a moment ago comes to the negative procedure from the truth in the name and on the way [*voie*] of which it raises the voice [*voix*]—the voice that speaks through its mouth: *alētheia* as the forgotten secret that sees itself thus unveiled or the truth as promised adequation. In any case, desire to say and rejoin what is *proper* to God.

—But what is this proper, if the proper of this proper consists in expropriating itself, if the proper of the proper *is* precisely, justly [*justement*], to have nothing of its own [*en propre*]? What does "is" mean here?

—Silesius never fails to expose, precisely, justly, the name of God [*justement*; for a re- and disadjustment of *justement* and "justice," see Derrida's *Spectres de Marx* (Paris: Galilee, 1993); *Specters of Marx: The State of the Debt, the Work of Mourning, and the New International*, trans. Peggy Kamuf (New York: Routledge, 1994)—Ed.].

> *Gottes Eigenschafft.*
> Was ist GOtts Eigenschafft? sich in Geschöpff ergiessen
> Allzeit derselbe seyn, nichts haben, wollen, wissen.*

God's own proper
What is God's own proper? to pour forth in creation,
To be the same in all times, to have, want, know nothing.*

(2: 132)

But the *post-scriptum* adds a decisive philosophical precision: a
remorse reinscribes this proposition within the ontology that opposes essence to accident, necessity to contingency:

*Understand this *accidentaliter* [*Verstehe* accidentaliter] or in a con-
tingent way [*oder zufälliger weise*]: for what God wants and knows, he
knows and wants essentially [*wesentlich*]. Thus he has nothing else (by
way of property [or quality: *mit Eigenschafft*]).

God "therefore no longer has anything" and, if he gives, as the
Good of Plotinus (*Enneads*, 6. 7-15-16-17), it is also what he does
not have, insofar as he is not only beyond being but also beyond his
gifts (*kai tou didomenou to didon epekeina ēn*). And to give is not to
engender, nor is it to *give birth.*

Now this revolution, at once interior and exterior, which makes
philosophy, onto-theological metaphysics, pass over the other edge
of itself, is also the condition of its translatability. What makes
philosophy go outside itself calls for a community that overflows its
tongue and broaches [*entame*] a process of universalization.

—What makes it go outside itself would come to it thus already
from the outside, from the absolute outside. That is why the
revolution could not be only internal [*intestine*].

—That's exactly what the revolution says, what the mystics and
the theologians of apophasis say when they speak of an absolute
transcendence that announces itself within. All that comes down to
the same or, indifferently, to the other. What we've just said about
philosophical Greece is also valid for the Greek tradition or translation of the Christian revelation. *On the one hand,* in the interior, if
one can say this, of a history of Christianity . . .

—But for a while now I have the impression that it is the idea itself of an identity or a self-interiority of every tradition (*the one* metaphysics, *the one* onto-theology, *the one* phenomenology, *the one* Christian revelation, *the one* history itself, *the one* history of being, *the one* epoch, *the one* tradition, self-identity in general, the one, etc.) that finds itself contested at its root.

—In effect, and negative theology is one of the most remarkable manifestations of this self-difference. Let's say then: in what one *could believe* to be the interior of a history of Christianity (and all that we have read of Silesius is through and through overdetermined by the themes of Christian revelation; other citations would have demonstrated this at any moment), the apophatic design is also anxious to render itself independent of revelation, of all the literal language of New Testament eventness [*événementialité*], of the coming of Christ, of the Passion, of the dogma of the Trinity, etc. An immediate but intuitionless mysticism, a sort of abstract kenōsis, frees this language from all authority, all narrative, all dogma, all belief—and at the limit from all faith. At the limit, this mysticism remains, after the fact [*après coup*], independent of all history of Christianity, *absolutely* independent, detached even, perhaps absolved, from the idea of sin, freed even, perhaps redeemed, from the idea of redemption. Whence the courage and the dissidence, potential or actual, of these masters (think of Eckhart), whence the persecution they suffered at times, whence their passion, whence this scent of heresy, these trials, this subversive marginality of the apophatic current in the history of theology and of the Church.

—Thus, what we were analyzing a while ago, this rupture of the social contract but as a process of universalization (in a way, a kind of spirit of the Enlightenment [*Lumières*]), is what would be regularly reproduced . . .

—You could almost say normally, inevitably, typically . . .

— . . . as dissidence or heresy, *pharmakos* to be excluded or sacrificed, another figure of passion. For it is true that, *on the other hand*, and according to the law of the same *double bind*, the dissident uprooting can claim to fulfill the vocation or the promise of Christianity in its most historic essence; thereby it responds to the call and to the gift of Christ, as it would resonate everywhere, in the ages of ages, rendering itself responsible for testifying before him, that is, before God (*Aufklärung* rather than Enlightenment, but let's leave . . .).

Besides, hidden or visible, metaphoric or literal (and with regard to the apophatic vigilance, this rhetoric on rhetoric moves itself as if into a state of dogmatic somnambulism), the reference to the Gospel is most often constitutive, ineffaceable, prescribed. Recall, for example, this "figure" of Christian interiorization that makes here of the heart a Mount of Olives, as Saint Paul speaks elsewhere of the circumcision of the heart:

> *Der Oelberg.*
> Sol dich deß Herren Angst erlösen von beschwerden,
> So muß dein Hertze vor zu einem Oelberg werden.
>
> *Mount of Olives*
> Should the Lord's agony redeem you of your sin,
> Your heart must become first a Mount of Olives.
>
> (2: 81)

—But don't you believe that a certain Platonism—or Neoplatonism—is indispensable and congenital here? "Plato, in order to dispose to Christianity" [*Pensées* 612/ 219], said Pascal, in whom one could at times discern the genius or the machine of apophatic dialectics . . .

—As is the case everywhere. And when Silesius names the eyes of the soul, how is one not to recognize there a vein of the Platonic *heritage*? But that can be found again elsewhere and without filiation. One can always affirm and deny a filiation; the affirmation or the assumption of this *inherited* debt as de-negation is the *double truth of filiation*, like that of negative theology.

—But isn't it more difficult to replatonize or rehellenize creationism? Now creationism often belongs to the logical structure of a good many apophatic discourses. In this way, creationism would also be their historic limit, in the double sense of this word: the limit *in* history and the limit *as* history. Like that of hell, the concept of creature is indispensable to Angelus Silesius. When he says to us, "Go there where you cannot go," it is to develop the title, in a way, of this maxim [*maxime*], to wit, "*GOtt ausser Creatur*," "God outside the creature" (1: 199). If the proper of God is not to have properties (He is everything save what He has), it is, as we heard, because God pours forth "in creation" (*ins Geschöpf*) . . .

—But what if that signified, in place of being a creationist dogma, that creation means expropriating production and that everywhere there is ex-appropriation there is creation? What if that were only a redefinition of the current concept of creation? Once more, one should say of no matter what or no matter whom what one says of God or some other thing: the thought of whomever concerning whomever or whatever, *it doesn't matter* [n'importe]. One would respond thus in the same way to the question "Who am I?" "Who are you?" "What is the other?" "What is anybody or anything as other?" "What is the being of beings [*l'être de l'étant*] as completely other?" All the examples are good ones, even if they all show that they are singularly though unequally good. The "no matter" of the "no matter whom" or of the "no matter what" would open the way to a sort of serene impassibility, to a very shrill insensibility, if I can put it this way, capable of being stirred by everything, precisely because of this element of indifference that opens onto no matter what difference. This is how I sometimes understand the tradition of *Gelâzenheit*, this serenity that allows for being without indifference, lets go without abandoning, unless it abandons without forgetting or forgets without forgetting—a se-

renity whose insistance one can trace from Meister Eckhardt to
Heidegger.[12]

—I have no objection to this hypothesis. As you describe this
Gelassenheit, you are very careful not to talk about love, and here
love is probably only a particular figure for all that this letting can
affect (without, however, affecting it). But why not recognize there
love itself, that is, this infinite renunciation which somehow *sur-*
renders to the impossible [se rend à l'impossible]? To surrender to the
other, and this is the impossible, would amount to giving oneself
over in going toward the other, to coming toward the other but
without crossing the threshold, and to respecting, to loving even
the invisibility that keeps the other inaccessible. To surrendering
one's weapons [*rendre les armes*]. (And *rendre* here no longer means
to restore or to reconstitute an integrity, to gather up in the pact or
in the symbolic.) To give oneself up [*se rendre*] and to surrender
one's weapons [*rendre les armes*] without defeat, without memory
or plan of war: so that this renunciation not be another ruse of
seduction or an added stratagem of jealousy. And everything would
remain intact—love, too, a love without jealousy that would allow
the other to be—after the passage of a *via negativa*. Unless I
interpret it too freely, this *via negativa* does not only constitute a
movement or a *moment* of deprivation, an asceticism or a provisional kenōsis. The deprivation should remain at work (thus give
up the work) for the (loved) other to remain the other. The other is
God or no matter whom, more precisely, no matter what singularity, as soon as any other is totally other [*tout autre est tout*
autre]. For the most difficult, indeed the impossible, resides there:
there where the other loses its name or can change it, to become no
matter what other. Passible and impassible, the *Gelassenheit* exerts
itself in us, it *is exerted* on this indifference by some other. It plays at
and plays with indifference, without playing. That explains, besides, if not a certain quietism, at least the role that *Gelassenheit*
plays in the thought of Silesius, and first of all the role that *play* itself
does not fail to play in the thought of divine creation:

GOtt spielt mit dem Geschöpffe.
Diß alles ist ein Spiel, das Jhr die GOttheit macht:
Sie hat die Creatur umb Jhret willn erdacht.

God plays with creation.
All that is play that the Deity gives Itself:
It has imagined the creature for Its pleasure.

(2: 198)

—Negative theology then can only present itself as one of the most playful forms of the creature's participation in this divine play, since "I" am "as" "God," you recall. There remains the question of what gives rise and place to this play, the question of the place opened for this play between God and his creation, in other terms, for ex-appropriation. In the maxim "*GOtt ausser Creatur*," the *adverb* that says the place (*wo*) gathers the whole enigma. Go [*Rendstoi*] there where you cannot go [*te rendre*], to the impossible, it is indeed the only way of going or coming. To go [*se rendre*] there where it is possible is not to surrender [*se rendre*], rather, it is to be already there and to paralyze oneself in the in-decision of the non-event [*anévénement*]:

Geh hin, wo du nicht kanst: sih, wo du sihest nicht:
Hör wo nichts schallt und klingt, so bestu wo Gott
    spricht.
(1: 199)

This adverb of place says the place (*wo*) of the word of God, of God as word, and "*Der Ort ist das Wort*" (1: 205) indeed affirms the place as word [*parole*] of God.

—Is this place created by God? Is it part of the play? Or else is it God himself? Or even what precedes, in order to make them possible, both God and his Play? In other words it remains to be known if this nonsensible (invisible and inaudible) place is opened by God, by the name of God (which would again be some other thing, perhaps), or if it is "older" than the time of creation, than

time itself, than history, narrative, word, etc. It remains to be
known (beyond knowing) if the place is opened by appeal (response, the event that calls for the response, revelation, history,
etc.), or if it remains impassively foreign, like *Khōra*, to everything
that takes its place and replaces itself and plays within this place,
including what is named God. Let's call this the test of *Khōra* . . .

—Do we have any choice? Why choose between the two? Is it
possible? But it is true that these two "places," these two experiences of place, these two ways are no doubt of an absolute heterogeneity. One place excludes the other, one (sur)passes the other,
one does without the other, one is, absolutely, *without* the other.
But what still relates them to each other is this strange preposition,
this strange with-without or without-with, *without* [English
in original—Ed.]. The logic of this junction or of this joining
(conjunction-disjunction) permits and forbids at once what could
be called exemplarism. Each thing, each being, you, me, the other,
each X, each name, and each name of God can become the example
of other substitutable X's. A process of absolute formalization. Any
other is totally other. [*Tout autre est tout autre.*] A name of God, in a
tongue, a phrase, a prayer, becomes an example of the name and of
names of God, then of names in general. *It is necessary* [*il faut*] to
choose *the best* of the examples (and it is necessarily the absolute
good, the *agathon*, which finds itself to be, then, *epekeina tēs
ousias*), but it is the best *as example*: for what it is and for what it is
not, for what it is and for what it represents, replaces, exemplifies.
And the "it is necessary" (the best) is also an example for all the "it
is necessary's" that there are and can be.

—*Il faut* does not only mean it is necessary, but, in French,
etymologically, "it lacks" or "is wanting." The lack or lapse is never
far away.

—This exemplarism joins and disjoins at once, dislocates the
best as the indifferent, the best as well as the indifferent: *on one side,*
on one way, a profound and abyssal eternity, fundamental but

accessible to messianism in general, to the teleo-eschatological narrative and to a certain experience or historical (or historial) revelation; *on the other side*, on the other way, the nontemporality of an abyss without bottom or surface, an absolute impassibility (neither life nor death) that gives rise to everything that it is not. In fact, two abysses.

—But the two abysses Silesius speaks about are two examples of the first abyss, the profound, the one that you have just defined first, although it is not in any way "first," precisely. Silesius writes:

> *Ein Abgrund rufft dem andern.*
> Der Abgrund meines Geists rufft immer mit Geschrey
> Den Abgrund GOttes an: sag welcher tieffer sey?
>
> *One abyss calls the other*
> The abyss of my spirit always invokes with cries
> The abyss of God: say which may be deeper?
>
> (1: 68)

—It is just this singular exemplarism that at once roots and uproots the idiom. Each idiom (for example, Greek onto-theology or Christian revelation) can testify for itself and for what it is not (not yet or forever), without this value of testimony (martyrdom) being itself totally determined by the inside of the idiom (Christian martyrdom, for example). There, in this testimony offered not to oneself but to the other, is produced the horizon of translatability— then of friendship, of universal community, of European decentering, beyond the values of *philia*, of charity, of everything that can be associated with them, even beyond the European interpretation of the name of Europe.

—Are you implying that it is on this condition that one can organize international and intercultural colloquiums on "negative theology"? (I would now put quotation marks around this expression.)

—For example. It is necessary in any case to think the historial and a-historial possibility of this project. Would you have imagined such a colloquium only a century ago? But what seems possible becomes thereby infinitely problematic. This double paradox resembles a double aporia: simultaneous negation and reaffirmation of Greek onto-theology and metaphysics, uprooting and expansion of Christianity, in Europe and outside of Europe, at the very moment when vocations, some statistics tell us, seem on the wane there . . .

—I am thinking of what is happening in Europe itself, in which the Pope appeals to the constitution or to the restoration of a Europe united in Christianity—which would be its very essence, and its destination. He tries to demonstrate, in the course of his voyages, that the victory over the totalitarianisms of the East has been carried off thanks to and in the name of Christianity. In the course of the so-called Gulf War, the allied western democracies often kept up a Christian discourse while speaking of international law. There would be too much to say here, and that is not the subject of the colloquium.

—On the one hand, this negation, as reaffirmation, can seem to double bolt the logocentric impasse of European domesticity (and India in this regard is not the absolute other of Europe). But on the other hand, it is also what, working on the *open* edge of this interiority or intimacy, *lets* [laisse] passage, *lets the other be*.

—*Laisser* is a difficult word to translate. How are they going to translate it? By "to leave," as in the phrase that won't be long in coming when we will shortly have to go our separate ways (I leave you, I am going, I *leave*) or else "to let"?

—Here we must have recourse to the German idiom. Silesius writes in the tradition of the *Gelassenheit* that, as we noted above, goes from Eckhart, at least, to Heidegger. It is necessary to leave all, to leave every "something" through love of God, and no doubt to leave God himself, to abandon him, that is, at once to leave him and (but) let him (be beyond being-something). Save his name [*sauf son nom*]—which must be kept silent there where it itself goes [*il se rend lui-même*] to *arrive* there, that is, to arrive at its own effacement.

> *Das etwas muß man lassen.*
> Mensch so du etwas liebst, so liebstu nichts fürwahr:
> GOtt ist nicht diß und das, drumb laß das Etwas gar.

> *One must leave the something*
> Man, if you love something, then you love nothing truly:
> God is not this and that, leave then forever the something.
>
> (1: 44)

Or again:

> *Die geheimste Gelassenheit.*
> Gelassenheit fäht GOtt: GOtt aber selbst zulassen,
> Jst ein Gelassenheit, die wenig Menschen fassen.

> *The most secret abandon*
> Abandon seizes God; but to leave God Himself,
> Is an abandonment that few men can grasp.
>
> (2: 92)

—The abandonment *of* this *Gelassenheit*, the abandonment *to* this *Gelassenheit* does not exclude pleasure or enjoyment; on the contrary, it gives rise to them. It opens the play *of* God (of God and with God, of God with self and with creation): it opens a passion to the enjoyment *of* God:

> *Wie kan man GOttes genissen.*
> GOtt ist ein Einges Ein, wer seiner wil geniessen,
> Muß sich nicht weniger als Er, in Jhn einschlissen.

> *How one can enjoy God*
> God is a Unique One; whoever wants to enjoy Him
> Must, no less than He, be enclosed in Him.
>
> (1: 83)

—To let passage to the other, to the totally other, is hospitality. A double hospitality: the one that has the form of Babel (the construction of the Tower, the appeal to universal translation, but also the violent imposition of the name, of the tongue, and of the idiom) *and* the one (another, the same) of the *deconstruction* of the Tower of Babel. The two designs are moved by a certain desire of universal community, beyond the desert of an arid formalization, that is, beyond economy itself. But the two must deal [*traiter*] with what they claim to avoid: the untreatable itself. The desire of God, God as the other name of desire, deals in the desert with radical atheism.

—In listening to you, one has more and more the feeling that *desert* is the other name, if not the proper place, of *desire*. And the at times oracular tone of apophasis, to which we alluded a few minutes ago, often resounds in a desert, which does not always come down to preaching in the desert.

—The movement toward the universal tongue oscillates between formalism, or the poorest, most arid, in effect the most desertlike techno-scientificity, and a sort of universal hive of inviolable secrets, of idioms that are never translated except as untranslatable seals. In this oscillation, "negative theology" is caught, comprised and comprehensive at once. But the Babelian narrative (construction and deconstruction at once) is still a (hi)story. Too full of sense. Here the invisible limit would pass less between the Babelian project and its deconstruction than between the Babelian place (event, *Ereignis*, history, revelation, eschato-teleology, messianism, address, destination, response and responsibility, construction and deconstruction) and "something" without thing, like an indeconstructible *Khōra*, the one that precedes itself in the test, as if they were two, the one and its double: the place that gives rise and place to Babel would be indeconstructible, not as a construction whose foundations would be sure, sheltered from every internal or external deconstruction, but as the very spacing of de-construction. There is where that happens and where there are those "things" called, for example, negative theology and its analogues, deconstruction and its analogues, this colloquium here and its analogues.

—What do you mean, by reassuring yourself in these "analogies"? That there is a singular chance in the transfer or the translation of that of which negative theology would be a sort of *analogon* or general equivalent, in the translatability uprooting but also returning this *analogon* to its Greek or Christian economy? That this chance would be that of a singularity doing today some other thing than losing itself in the community?

—Perhaps. But I would not yet speak of human, nor even anthropotheocentric, community or singularity, nor even of a *Gevier* in which what is called "animal" would be a mortal passed over in silence. Yes, the *via negativa* would perhaps today be the passage of the idiom into the most common desert, as the chance of law [*droit*] and of another treaty of universal peace (beyond what is today called international law, that thing very positive but still so tributary of the European concept of the State and of law, then so easy to arraign [*arraisonner*] for particular States): the chance of a promise and of an announcement in any case.

—Would you go so far as to say that today there is a "politics" and a "law" of negative theology? A juridico-political lesson to be drawn from the possibility of this theology?

—No, not to be drawn, not to be deduced as from a program, from premises or axioms. But there would no more be any "politics," "law," or "morals" *without* this possibility, the very possibility that obliges us from now on to place these words between quotation marks. Their sense will have trembled.

—But you admit at the same time that "without" and "not without" [*pas sans*] are the most difficult words to say and to hear/understand, the most unthinkable or most impossible. What does Silesius mean, for example, when he leaves us the *inheritance* of this maxim:

> *Kein Tod ist ohn ein Leben.*
> *No death is without life*
> (1: 36)

and better:

> *Nichts lebet ohne Sterben.*
> GOtt selber, wenn Er dir wil leben, muß er sterben:
> Wie dänckstu ohne Tod sein Leben zuererben?
>
> *Nothing lives without dying*
> God himself, If He wants to live for you, must die:
> How do you think, without death, to inherit his own life?
>
> (1: 33)

—Has anything more profound ever been written on inheritance? I understand that as a thesis on what *inherit* means (to say). Both to give the name and to receive it. Save [*Sauf,* Safe]—

—Yes, as the "without," heritage, inheritance, filiation, if you prefer, is the most difficult thing to think and to "live," to "die." But don't forget that these maxims of Silesius, notably those that immediately surround them (1: 30, 31, 32, 34, etc.), have a Christian sense, and the *post-scripta* of maxims 31 and 32 ("*God dies and lives in us* / I do not die or live: God himself dies in me," etc.) cite Saint Paul in order to explain how it is necessary to read. They teach how to read by reading Saint Paul, and not otherwise. A *post-scriptum* of Christian reading or self-interpretation can command the whole perspective of the *Cherubinic Wanderer,* and of all the "without's", including "*GOtt mag nichts ohne mich*" (1: 96), including "*GOtt ist ohne Willen*" (1: 294), and including, whether Heidegger likes it or not, the "*Ohne warumb*" of "Die Ros' ist ohn warumb" (1: 289). If Heidegger doesn't like this, it is necessary for him to write another *post-scriptum,* which is always possible, and represents another experience of inheritance.

The difficulty of the "without" spreads into what is still called politics, morals, or law, which are just as threatened as promised by apophasis. Take the example of democracy, of the idea of democracy, of democracy to come (neither the Idea in the Kantian sense, nor the current, limited, and determined concept of democracy, but democracy as the inheritance of a promise). Its path passes perhaps today in the world through (across) the aporias of negative theology that we just analyzed so schematically.

—How can a path pass through aporias?

—What would a path be without aporia? Would there be a way [*voie*] without what clears the way there where the way is not opened, whether it is blocked or still buried in the nonway? I cannot think the notion of the way without the necessity of deciding there where the decision seems impossible. Nor can I think the decision and thus the responsibility there where the decision is already possible and programmable. And would one speak, could one only speak of this thing? Would there be a voice [*voix*] for that? A name?

—You recognize that the possibility, then, of speaking or walking seems just as impossible. So difficult in any case that this passage through aporia seems first of all (perhaps) reserved as a secret for a few. This esoterism seems strange for a democracy, even for this democracy to come that you define no more than apophasis defines God. Its to-come would be jealously thought, watched over, hardly taught by a few. Very suspect.

—Understand me, it's a matter of maintaining a double injunction. Two concurrent desires divide apophatic theology, at the edge of nondesire, around the gulf and chaos of the *Khōra*: the desire to be inclusive of all, thus understood by all (community, *koinē*) and the desire to keep or entrust the secret within the very strict limits of those who hear/understand it *right*, as secret, and are then capable or worthy of keeping it. The secret, no more than democracy or the secret of democracy, must not, besides, cannot, be entrusted to the inheritance of no matter whom. Again the paradox of the example: the no-matter-who (any example sample) must also give the *good* example. Understand me when I say that, I am still citing Silesius, in this sort of *post-scriptum* that he adds to the maxim on "*The blessed silence (Das seelige Stilleschweigen)*" (1: 19). It is a matter of rightly understanding a silence, as elsewhere, the *Gelassenheit*: "Wie seelig ist der Mensch, der weder wil noch weiß!"; "How blessed the man who neither wishes nor knows!" And here is the Nota Bene as *post-scriptum*: "Der GOtt (versteh mich recht) nicht gibet Lob noch Preiß"; "To God (understand me right) give neither praise nor glory." And you remember that "few men" are ready to grasp the exemplary *Gelassenheit*, the one that not only grasps, but knows how to abandon God (2: 92). The reserved, the most refined, the rarest secret is that of one *Gelassenheit* and not of the other, of this *Gelassenheit* here and not of another that resembles it, of this leaving-the-other-here and not of the other. From where would this serenity of abandonment be given (by what? by whom?), this serenity which would also be understood, beyond all knowledge, as not giving anything to God [*à Dieu*], not even Adieu, not even to his name.

—To give a name, is that still to give? Is that to give some thing? And something ever other than a sur-name, such as God or *Khōra,* for example . . .

—One can have doubts about it from the moment when the name not only is nothing, in any case is not the "thing" that it names, not the "nameable" or the renowned, but also risks to bind, to enslave or to engage the other, to link the called, to call him/her to respond even before any decision or any deliberation, even before any freedom. An assigned passion, a prescribed alliance as much as a promise. And still, if the name never belongs originarily and rigorously to s/he who receives it, it also no longer belongs from the very first moment to s/he who gives it. According to a formula that haunts our tradition from Plotinus to Heidegger, who does not cite him, and to Lacan, who cites neither the former nor the latter,[13] and better than ever, the gift of the name gives that which it does not have, that in which, prior to everything, may consist the essence, that is to say—beyond being—the nonessence, of the gift.

—One last question. One may foresee it better, Angelus Silesius does not represent the whole, nor even the best example of "classic" or canonic negative theology. Why bring everything back to him?

—Here you have to believe in the accident or in the contingency of a (hi)story: an autobiographical chance [*aléa*], if you like, that is happening to me this summer. I chose to bring here with me this given book, the *Cherubinic Wanderer* (and only extracts at that), to bring it to this family place, in order to watch over a mother who is slowly leaving us and no longer knows how to name. As unknown as he remains to me, Silesius begins to be more familiar and more friendly to me. I have been coming back to him recently, almost secretly, because of sentences that I have not cited today. And furthermore, it takes up little room when one is traveling (seventy pages). Isn't negative theology—we have said this enough—also the most economical formalization? The greatest power of the possible? A reserve of language, almost inexhaustible in so few words? This literature forever elliptical, taciturn, cryptic, obstinately withdrawing, however, from all literature, inaccessible there even where it seems to go [*se rendre*], the exasperation of a jealousy that passion carries beyond itself; this would seem to be a literature for the desert or for exile. It holds desire in suspense, and always saying too much or too little, each time it leaves you without ever going away from you.

TRANSLATED BY JOHN P. LEAVEY, JR.

KHŌRA

Thus myth puts in play a form of logic which could be called—in contrast to the logic of noncontradiction of the philosophers—a logic of the ambiguous, of the equivocal, of polarity. How can one formulate, or even formalize, these see-saw operations, which flip any term into its opposite whilst at the same time keeping them both apart, from another point of view? The mythologist was left with drawing up, in conclusion, this statement of deficit, and to turn to the linguists, logicians, mathematicians, that they might supply him with the tool he lacked: the structural model of a logic which would not be that of binarity, of the yes or no, a logic other than the logic of the *logos*.

—Jean-Pierre Vernant, "Raisons du mythe," *Mythe et societé en Grèce ancienne* (Paris, 1974), p. 250.

§ *Khōra*

Khōra reaches us, and as the name. And when a name comes, it immediately says more than the name: the other of the name and quite simply the other, whose irruption the name announces. This announcement does not yet promise, no more than it threatens. It neither promises nor threatens anyone. It still remains alien to the person, only naming imminence, even only an imminence that is alien to the myth, the time, and the history of every possible promise and threat.

It is well known: what Plato in the *Timaeus* designates by the name of *khōra* seems to defy that "logic of noncontradiction of the philosophers" of which Vernant speaks, that logic "of binarity, of the yes or no." Hence it might perhaps derive from that "logic other than the logic of the *logos.*" The *khōra*, which is neither "sensible" nor "intelligible," belongs to a "third genus" (*triton genos*, 48a, 52a). One cannot even say of it that it is *neither* this *nor* that or that it is *both* this *and* that. It is not enough to recall that *khōra* names neither this nor that, or, that *khōra* says this and that. The difficulty declared by Timaeus is shown in a different way: at times the *khōra* appears to be neither this nor that, at times both this and that, but this alternation between the logic of exclusion and that of participation—we shall return to this at length—stems perhaps only from a provisional appearance and from the constraints of rhetoric, even from some incapacity for naming.

The *khōra* seems to be alien to the order of the "paradigm," that intelligible and immutable model. And yet, "invisible" and without sensible form, it "participates" in the intelligible in a very troublesome and indeed aporetic way (*aporōtata*, 51b). At least we shall not be lying, adds Timaeus, at least we shall not be saying what is false (*ou pseudometha*) in declaring this. The prudence of this negative formulation gives reason to ponder. Not lying, not saying what is false: is this necessarily telling the truth? And, in this respect, what about testimony, bearing witness [*témoignage*]?

Let us recall once more, under the heading of our preliminary approach, that the discourse on the *khōra*, as it is *presented*, does not proceed from the natural or legitimate *logos*, but rather from a hybrid, bastard, or even corrupted reasoning (*logismō nothō*). It comes "as in a dream" (52b), which could just as well deprive it of lucidity as confer upon it a power or divination.

Does such a discourse derive, then, from myth? Shall we gain access to the thought of the *khōra* by continuing to place our trust in the alternative *logos/mythos*? And what if this thought called *also* for a third genus of discourse? And what if, perhaps as in the case of the *khōra*, this appeal to the third genre was only the moment of a detour in order to signal toward a genre beyond genre? Beyond categories, and above all beyond categorial oppositions, which in the first place allow it to be approached or said?

As a token of gratitude and admiration, here then is homage in the form of a question to Jean-Pierre Vernant. The question is addressed to the one who taught us so much and gave us so much pause for thought about the opposition *mythos/ logos*, certainly, but also about the unceasing inversion of poles; to the author of "Raisons du mythe" and of *Ambiguïté et renversement*: how are we to think that which, while going outside of the regularity of the *logos*, its law, its natural or legitimate genealogy, nevertheless does not belong, *stricto sensu*, to *mythos*? Beyond the retarded or johnny-come-lately opposition of *logos* and *mythos*, how is one to think the necessity of that which, while *giving place* to that opposition as to so many others, seems sometimes to be itself no longer subject to the law of the very thing which it *situates*? What of this *place*? It is nameable? And wouldn't it have some impossible relation to the possibility of naming? Is there something to *think* there, as I have just so hastily said, and to think according to *necessity*?

I

The oscillation of which we have just spoken is not an oscillation among others, an oscillation between two poles. It oscillates between two types of oscillation: the double exclusion (*neither/nor*) and the participation (*both this and that*). But have we the right to transport the logic, the para-logic or the meta-logic of this super-oscillation from one set to the other? It concerned first of all types of existent thing (sensible/intelligible, visible/invisible, form/formless, icon, or mimeme/paradigm), but we have displaced it toward types of discourse (*mythos/logos*) or of relation to what is or is not in general. No doubt such a displacement is not self-evident. It depends on a sort of metonymy: such a metonymy would displace itself, by displacing the names, from types [*genres*] of being to types [*genres*] of discourse. But on the one hand it is always difficult, particularly in Plato, to separate the two problematics: the quality of the discourse depends primarily on the quality of the being of which it speaks. It is almost as if a name should only be given to whom (or to what) deserves it and calls for it. The discourse, like the relation to that which is in general, is qualified or disqualified by what it relates to. On the other hand, the metonymy is authorized by passing through *genre*, from one genre to the other, from the question of the genres/types of being to the question of the types of discourse. Now the discourse on the *khōra* is also a discourse on genre/type (*genos*) and on different types of type. Later we will get on to genre as *gens*, or people (*genos, ethnos*), a theme which appears at the opening of the *Timaeus*. In the narrow context on which we are dwelling at present, that of the sequence on the *khōra*, we shall encounter two further genres of genre or types of type. The *khōra* is a *triton genos* in view of the two types of being (immutable and intelligible/corruptible, in the process of becoming and sensible), but it seems to be equally determined with regard to the sexual type: Timaeus speaks of "mother" and "nurse" in regard to this subject. He does this in a mode which we shall not be in a hurry to name. Almost all the interpreters of the *Timaeus* gamble here on the resources of rhetoric without ever wondering about them. They speak tranquilly about metaphors, images, similes.[1] They ask themselves no questions about this tradition of rhetoric which places at their disposal a reserve of concepts which are very useful but which are all built upon this distinction between the sensible and the intelligible, which is precisely what the thought of the *khōra* can no longer get along with—a distinction, indeed, of which Plato unambiguously lets it be known that this thought has the greatest difficulty getting along with it. This problem of rhetoric—particularly of the possibility of naming—is, here, no mere side issue. Nor is its importance limited to some pedagogic, illustrative, or instrumental dimension (those who speak of metaphor with regard to the *khōra* often add: didactic metaphor). We shall be content for the moment with indicating it, and situating it, but it is already clear that, just like the *khōra* and with just as much necessity, it cannot easily be situated, assigned to a residence: it is more situating than situated, an opposition which must in its turn be shielded from some grammatical or ontological alternative between the active and the passive. We shall not speak of metaphor, but not in order to hear, for example, that the *khōra is properly* a mother, a nurse, a receptacle, a bearer of imprints or gold. It is perhaps because its scope goes beyond or falls short of the polarity of metaphorical sense versus proper sense that the thought of the *khōra* exceeds the polarity, no doubt analogous, of the *mythos* and the *logos*. Such at least would be the question which we should like here to put to the test of a reading. The consequence which we envisage would be the following: with these two polarities, the thought of the *khōra* would trouble the very order of polarity, of polarity in general, whether dialectical or not. Giving place to oppositions, it would itself not submit to any reversal. And this, which is another consequence, would not be because it would inalterably be *itself* beyond its name but because in carrying beyond the polarity of sense (metaphorical or proper), it would no longer belong to the horizon of sense, nor to that of meaning as the meaning of being.

After these precautions and these negative hypotheses, you will understand why it is that we left the name *khōra* sheltered from any translation. A translation, admittedly, seems to be always at work, both *in* the Greek language and from the Greek language into some other. Let us not regard any of them as sure. Thinking and translating here traverse the same experience. If it must be attempted, such an experience or experiment [*expérience*] is not only but of concern for a word or an atom of meaning but also for a whole tropological texture, let us not yet call it a system, and for ways of approaching, in order to *name* them, the elements of this "tropology." Whether they concern the word *khōra* itself ("place," "location," "region," "country") or what tradition calls the figures—comparisons, images, and metaphors—proposed by Timaeus ("mother," "nurse," "receptable," "imprint-bearer"), the translations remain caught in networks of interpretation. They are led astray by retrospective projections, which can always be suspected of being anachronistic. This anachronism is not necessarily, not always, and not only a weakness from which a vigilant and rigorous interpretation would be able to escape entirely. We shall try to show that no-one escapes from it. Even Heidegger, who is nonetheless one of the only ones never to speak of "metaphor," seems to us to yield to this teleological retrospection,[2] against which, elsewhere, he so rightly puts us on our guard. And this gesture seems highly significant for the whole of his questioning and his relationship to the "history-of-philosophy."

What has just been said of rhetoric, of translation, or of teleological anachronism, could give rise to a misunderstanding. We must dispel it without delay. We would never claim to propose the exact word, the *mot juste*, for *khōra*, nor to name it, *itself*, over and above all the turns and detours of rhetoric, nor finally to approach it, *itself*, for what it will have been, outside of any point of view, outside of any anachronic perspective. Its name is not an exact word, not a *mot juste*. It is promised to the ineffaceable even if what it names, *khōra*, is not reduced to its name. Tropology and anachronism are inevitable. And all we would like to show is that it is structure which makes them thus inevitable, makes of them something other than accidents, weaknesses, or provisional moments. It is this structural law which seems to me never to have been approached *as such* by the whole history of interpretations of the *Timaeus*. It would be a matter of a structure and not of some essence of the *khōra*, since the question or essence no longer has any meaning with regard to it. Not having an essence, how could the *khōra* be [*se tiendrait-elle*] beyond its name? The *khōra* is anachronistic; it "is" the anachrony within being, or better: the anachrony of being. It anachronizes being.

The "whole history of interpretations," we have just said. We will never exhaust the immense literature devoted to the *Timaeus* since antiquity. It is out of the question to deal with it here in its entirety. And, above all, to presuppose the unity or homogeneity of this whole, the very possibility of totalizing it in some ordered apprehension. What we shall presuppose, by contrast, and one could still call it a "working hypothesis," is that the presumption of such an order (grouping, unity, totality organized by a *telos*) has an essential link with the structural anachronism of which we spoke a moment ago. It would be the inevitable effect produced by *something like* the *khōra*—which is not something, and which is not *like* anything, not even like what *it* would be, *itself*, there beyond its name.

Rich, numerous, inexhaustible, the interpretations come, in short, to give form to the meaning of *khōra*. They always consist in *giving form* to it by determining it, it which, however, can "offer itself" or promise itself only by removing itself from any determination, from all the marks or impressions to which we say it is exposed: from everything which we would like to give to it without hoping to receive anything from it . . . But what we are putting forward here of the interpretation of the *khōra*—of Plato's text on the *khōra*—by speaking about a form given or received, about mark or impression, about knowledge as information, etc., all of that already draws on what the text itself says about the *khōra*, draws on its conceptual and hermeneutic apparatus. What we have just put forward, for example, for the sake of the example, on the subject of "*khōra*" in the text of Plato, reproduces or simply brings back, with all its schemas, Plato's discourse on the subject of the *khōra*. And this is true even down to this very sentence in which I have just made use of the word *schemas*. The *skhemata* are the cut-out figures imprinted into the *khōra*, the forms which inform it. They are of it without belonging to it.

Thus there are interpretations which would come to give form to "*khōra*" by leaving on it the schematic mark of their imprint and by depositing on it the sediment of their contribution. And yet, "*khōra*" seems never to let itself be reached or touched, much less broached, and above all not exhausted by these *types* of tropological or interpretative translation. One cannot even say that it furnishes them with the support of a stable substratum or substance. *Khōra* is not a subject. It is not the subject. Nor the support [*subjectile*]. The hermeneutic *types* cannot inform, they cannot give form to *khōra* except to the extent that, inaccessible, impassive, "amorphous" (*amorphon*, 51a) and still virgin, with a virginity that is radically rebellious against anthropomorphism, it *seems to receive* these types and *give place* to them. But if Timaeus names it as receptacle (*dekhomenon*) or place (*khōra*), these names do not designate an essence, the stable being of an *eidos*, since *khōra* is neither of the order of the *eidos* nor of the order of mimemes, that is, of images of the *eidos* which come to imprint themselves in it—which thus *is not* and does not belong to the two known or recognized genera of being. It is not, and this nonbeing cannot but be *declared*, that is, be caught or conceived, via the anthropomorphic schemas of the verb *to receive* and the verb *to give*. *Khōra* is not, is above all not, is anything but a support or a subject which would *give* place by receiving or by conceiving, or indeed by letting itself be conceived. How could one deny it this essential significance as a receptacle, given that this very name is given to it by Plato? It is difficult indeed, but perhaps we have not yet thought through what is meant by *to receive*, the receiving of the receptacle, what is said by *dekhomai, dekhomenon*. Perhaps it is from *khōra* that we are beginning to learn it—to receive it, to receive from it what its name calls up. To receive it, if not to comprehend it, to conceive it.

You will already have noticed that we now say *khōra* and not, as convention has always required, *the khōra*, or again, as we might have done for the sake of caution, the word, the concept, the significance, or the value of "*khōra.*" This is for several reasons, most of which are no doubt already obvious. The definite article presupposes the existence of a thing, the existent *khōra* to which, via a common name [*nom commun*, or "common noun"—Ed.], it would be easy to refer. But what is said about *khōra* is that this name does not designate any of the known or recognized or, if you like, received types of existent, *received* by philosophical discourse, that is, by the *ontological logos* which lays down the law in the *Timaeus*: *khōra* is neither sensible nor intelligible. There is *khōra*; one can even ponder its *physis* and its *dynamis*, or at least ponder these in a preliminary way. But what *there is*, there, is not; and we will come back later to what this *there is* can give us to think, this *there is*, which, by the way, *gives* nothing in giving place or in giving to think, whereby it will be risky to see in it the equivalent of an *es gibt*, of the *es gibt* which remains without a doubt implicated in every negative theology, unless it is the *es gibt* which always summons negative theology in its Christian history.

Instead of *the khōra*, shall we be content to say prudently: the word, the common name, the concept, the signification, or the value of *khōra*? These precautions would not suffice; they presuppose distinctions (word/concept, word-concept/thing, meaning/reference, signification/value, etc.) which themselves imply the possibility, at least, of a *determined* existent, distinct from another, and acts which aim at it, at it or its meaning, via acts of language, designations or sign postings. All of these acts appeal to generalities, to an *order* of multiplicities: genus, species, individual, type, schema, etc. Now what we can read, it seems, of *khōra* in the *Timaeus* is that "something," which is not a thing, puts in question these presuppositions and these distinctions: "something" is not a thing and escapes from this order of multiplicities.

But if we say *khōra* and not *the khōra*, we are still making a name out of it. A proper name, it is true, but a word, just like any common name, a word distinct from the thing or the concept. Besides, the proper name appears, as always, to be attributed to a person, in this case to a woman. Perhaps to a woman; indeed, to a woman. Doesn't that aggravate the risks of anthropomorphism against which we wanted to protect ourselves? Aren't these risks run by Plato himself when he seems to "compare," as they say, *khōra* to a mother or a nurse? Isn't the value of receptacle also associated, like passive and virgin matter, with the feminine element, and precisely in Greek culture? These objections are not without value. However, if *khōra* indeed presents certain attributes of the word as proper name, isn't that only via its apparent reference to some uniqueness (and in the *Timaeus*, more rigorously in a certain passage of the *Timaeus* which we will approach later, there is *only one khōra*, and that is indeed how we understand it; there is only one, however divisible it be), the referent or this reference does not exist. It does not have the characteristics of an existent, by which we mean an existent that would be receivable in the *ontologic*, that is, those of an intelligible *or* sensible existent. There is *khōra* but *the khōra* does not exist. The effacement of the article should for the moment suspend the determination, within invisible quotation marks (we cite a saying of Plato's in a certain passage of the *Timaeus*, without knowing yet what it means and how to determine it) and the reference to something which is not a thing but which insists, in its so enigmatic uniqueness, lets itself be called or causes itself to be named without answering, without giving itself to be seen, conceived, determined. Deprived of a real referent, that which in fact resembles a proper name finds itself also called an X which has as its property (as its *physis* and as its *dynamis*, Plato's text will say) that it has nothing as its own and that it remains unformed, formless (*amorphon*). This very singular impropriety, which precisely is nothing, is just what *khōra* must, if you like, *keep*; it is just what *must be kept for it*, what *we* must keep for it. To that end, it is necessary not to confuse it in a generality by properly attributing to it properties which would still be those of a determinate existent, one of the existents which it/she "receives" or whose image it/she receives: for example, an existent of the female gender—and that is why the femininity of the mother or the nurse will never be attributed to it/her as a property, something of her own. Which does not mean, however—we shall return to this—that it is a case here of mere figures of rhetoric. *Khōra* must not receive for *her own sake*, so she must not *receive*, merely let herself be lent the properties (of that) which she receives. She must not receive, she must receive not that which she receives. To avoid all these confusions, it is convenient, paradoxically, to formalize our approach (to it/her) and always to use the same language about it/her ("ταὐτόν αὐτὴν ἀεὶ προσρητέον," 50b). Not so much to "give her always the same name," as it is often translated, but to speak of it/her and to call it/her *in the same manner*. In short, faithfully even if this *faith* is irreducible to every other. Is this "manner" unique or typical? Does it have the singularity of an idiomatic event or the regulated generality of a schema? In other words, does this regularity find, in Plato's text, or rather in a particular passage of the *Timaeus*, its unique and best formulation, or rather one of its examples, however privileged? In what regard, in what sense, will it be said of the *Timaeus* that it is exemplary? And if it is important that the *appellation*, rather than the *name*, should stay the same, will we be able to replace, relay, translate *khōra* by other names, striving only to preserve the regularity of the appellation, namely of a discourse?

This question cannot but resound when we know that we are caught in such a scene of reading, included in advance in the immense history of interpretations and reappropriations which in the course of the centuries come to buzz and hum around *khōra*, taking charge of it/her or overloading it/her with inscriptions and reliefs, giving it/her form, imprinting it/her with types, in order to produce in it/her new objects or to deposit on it/her other sediments [the translation of the French pronoun *elle*, referring to *khōra*, includes both "her" and "it," in order to stress that *elle* could also be understood as a personal feminine pronoun—Ed.]. This interminable theory of exegeses seems to reproduce what, following the discourse of Timaeus, would happen, not with Plato's text, but with *khōra* herself/itself. With *khōra itself/herself*, if one could at all speak thus about this X (χ or *khi*) which must not have any proper determination, sensible or intelligible, material or formal, and therefore must not have any identity of its/her own, must not be identical with herself/itself. *Everything happens as if* the yet-to-come history of the interpretations of *khōra* were written or even prescribed in advance, *in advance reproduced and reflected* in a few pages of the *Timaeus* "on the subject" of *khōra* "herself" ("itself"). With its ceaseless re-launchings, its failures, its superimpositions, its overwritings and reprintings, this history wipes itself out in advance since it programs itself, reproduces itself, and reflects itself by anticipation. Is a prescribed, programmed, reproductive, reflexive history still a history? Unless the concept of history bears within itself this teleological programming which annuls it while constituting it. In saying, in short, "this is how one can glimpse *khōra*—in a difficult, aporetical way and as if in a dream—," someone (Timaeus, Plato, etc.) would have said: this is what henceforth all the interpretations, for all eternity, of what I say here will look like. They will resemble *what I am saying* about *khōra*; and hence what I am saying about *khōra* gives a commentary, in advance, and describes the law of the whole history of the hermeneutics and the institutions which will be constructed *on this subject*, over this subject.

There is nothing fortuitous about that. *Khōra* receives, so as to give place to them, all the determinations, but she/it does not possess any of them as her/its own. She possesses them, she has them, since she receives them, but she does not possess them as properties, she does not possess anything as her own. She "is" nothing other than the sum or the process of what has just been inscribed "on" her, on the subject of her, on her subject, right up against her subject, but she is not the *subject* or the *present support* of all these interpretations, even though, nevertheless, she is not reducible to them. Simply this excess is nothing, nothing that may be and be said ontologically. This absence of support, which cannot be translated into absent support or into absence as support, provokes *and* resists any binary or dialectical determination, any inspection of a philosophical *type*, or let us say, more rigorously, of an *ontological* type. This type finds itself both defied and re-launched by the very thing that appears to give it place. Even then we shall have to recall later, insisting on it in a more analytical manner, that *if there is place*, or, according to our idiom, *place given*, to give place here does not come to the same thing as to make a present of a place. The expression *to give place* does not refer to the gesture of a donor-subject, the support or origin of something which would come to be given to someone.

Despite their timidly preliminary character, these remarks per-mit us perhaps to glimpse the silhouette of a "logic" which seems virtually impossible to formalize. Will this "logic" still be a logic, "a form of logic," to take up Vernant's saying when he speaks of a "form of logic" of myth which must be "formulated, or even formalized"? Such a logic of myth exists, no doubt, but our ques-tion returns: does the thought of *khōra*, which obviously does not derive from the "logic of noncontradiction of the philosophers," belong to the space of mythic thought? Is the "bastard" *logos* which is regulated according to it [i.e., according to mythic thought—Tr.]—still a *mythos*?

Let us take the time for a long detour. Let us consider the manner in which Hegel's speculative dialectic inscribes mythic thought in a teleological perspective. One can say of this dialectic that it is and that it is not a logic of noncontradiction. It integrates and *sublates* contradiction as such. In the same way, it sublates mythic discourse as such into the philosopheme.

According to Hegel, philosophy becomes serious—and we are also thinking *after* Hegel and *according to* him, following his thought—only from the moment when it enters into the sure path of logic: that is, after having abandoned, or let us rather say sublated, its mythic *form*: after Plato, with Plato. Philosophical logic comes to its senses when the concept wakes up from its mythological slumber. Sleep and waking, for the event, consist in a simple unveiling: the making explicit and taking cognizance of a philosopheme enveloped in its virtual potency. The mytheme *will have been* only a prephilosopheme offered and promised to a dialectical *Aufhebung*. This teleological future anterior resembles the time of a narrative but it is a narrative of the going outside of narrative. It marks the end of narrative fiction. Hegel explains it[3] while defending his "friend Creuzer" and his book, *Symbolism and Mythology of Ancient Peoples, especially of the Greeks* (1810–12). The mythological *logos*, of course, can emit the pretension of being a species of "philosophizing" (p. 108). There are philosophers who have used myths in order to bring philosophemes closer to the imagination (*Phantasie*). But "the content of myth is thought" (*ibid.*). The mythic dimension remains formal and exterior. If Plato's myths are "beautiful," one would be wrong to think that myths are more "eminent" (*vortrefflicher*) than the "abstract mode of expression." In truth, Plato has recourse to myth only to the extent of his "impotence" (*Unvermögen*) to "express himself in the pure modality of thought." But that is also in part because he does so only in the introduction to the dialogues—and an introduction is never purely philosophical: you know what Hegel thinks of introductions and prefaces in general. When he gets on to the thing itself, to the principal subject, Plato expresses himself quite otherwise. Let us think of the *Parmenides*, for example: the simple determinations of thought do without image and myth. Hegel's dialectical schema here just as much concerns the mythic—the figurative or the symbolic. The *Parmenides* is "serious," whereas the recourse to myth is not entirely so. In the form in which, still today, this opposition dominates so many evaluations—and not only in so-called Anglo-Saxon thought—the opposition between the serious and the nonserious overlaps here with that of philosophy *as such* and of its ludico-mythological drift [*dérive*]. The *value* of philosophical thought, which is also to say its *seriousness*, is measured by the nonmythic character of its terms. Hegel here emphasizes value, seriousness, the value of seriousness, and Aristotle is his guarantor. For after having declared that "the value of Plato, however, does not reside in myths" ("der Wert Platons liegt aber nicht in den Mythen," p. 109), Hegel quotes and translates Aristotle. It is appropriate to dwell on this. We know, let us recall in passing before approaching this problem directly, how great a weight the Aristotelian interpretation of the *Timaeus* carries in the history of the interpretations. Hegel translates then, or paraphrases, the *Metaphsics*:

περι μὲν τῶν μυτικῶς σοφιζομένων οὐκ ἀξιον μετὰ σπουδῆς σκοπεῖν

Von denen, welche mythisch philosophieren, ist es nicht der Mühe wert, ernstlich zu handeln.

Those who philosophize with recourse to myth are not worth treating seriously.

Hegel seems to oscillate between two interpretations. In a philosophical text, the function of myth is at times a sign of philosophical impotence, the incapacity to accede to the concept as such and to keep to it, at other times the index of a dialectic and above all didactic potency, the pedagogic mastery of the serious philosopher in full possession of the philosopheme. Simultaneously or successively, Hegel seems to recognize in Plato both this impotence and this mastery. These two evaluations are only apparently contradictory or are so only up to a certain point. They have this in common: the subordination of myth, as a discursive *form*, to the *content* of the signified concept, to the meaning, which, in its essence, can only be philosophical. And the philosophical theme, the signified concept, whatever may be its formal *presentation*—philosophical or mythic—always remains the force of law, the mastery or the dynasty of discourse. Here one can see the thread of our question passing by: if *khōra* has no meaning or essence, if she is not a philosopheme and if, nevertheless, she is neither the object nor the form of a fable of a mythic type, where can she be situated in this schema?

Apparently contradictory, but in fact profoundly coherent, this logico-philosophical evaluation is not *applied* to Plato. It derives already from a certain "Platonism." Hegel does not read Plato through Aristotle as if doing something unknown to Plato, as if he [Hegel] were deciphering a practice whose meaning would have remained inaccessible to the author of the *Timaeus*. A certain programme of this evaluation seems already legible in this work, as we shall verify. But perhaps with one reservation, and this supplementary reservation could lodge, shelter, and thereby exceed the said programme.

First, the programme. The cosmogony of the *Timaeus* runs through the cycle of knowledge on all things. Its encyclopedic end must mark the term, the *telos*, of a *logos* on the subject of everything that is: "καὶ δὴ καὶ τέλος περὶ τοῦ παντὸς νῦν ἤδη τὸν λόγον ἡμῖν φῶμεν ἔχειν"; "And now at length we may say that our discourse concerning the Universe has reached its termination" (92c).

This encyclopedic *logos* is a general ontology, treating of all the types of being, it includes a theology, a cosmology, a physiology, a psychology, a zoology. Mortal or immortal, human and divine, visible and invisible things are situated there. By recalling it in conclusion, one picks up the distinction between the visible living thing, for example, the sensible god, and the intelligible god of which it is the image (*eikōn*). The cosmos is the heavens (*ouranos*) as living, visible thing and sensible god. It is unique and alone of its race, "monogenic."

And yet, half-way through the cycle, won't the discourse on *khōra* have opened, between the sensible and the intelligible, belonging neither to one nor to the other, hence neither to the cosmos as sensible god nor to the intelligible god, an apparently empty space—even though it is no doubt not *emptiness*? Didn't it name a gaping opening, an abyss or a chasm? Isn't it starting out from this chasm, "in" it, that the cleavage between the sensible and the intelligible, indeed, between body and soul, can have place and take place? Let us not be too hasty about bringing this chasm named *khōra* close to that chaos which also opens the yawning gulf of the abyss. Let us avoid hurling into it the anthropomorphic form and the pathos of fright. Not in order to install in its place the security of a foundation, the "exact counterpart of what Gaia represents for any creature, since her appearance, at the origin of the world: a stable foundation, sure for all eternity, opposed to the gaping and bottomless opening of Chaos."[4] We shall later encounter a brief allusion of Heidegger's to *khōra*, not to the one in the

Timaeus but, outside of all quotation and all precise reference, the one which in Plato would designate the place (*Ort*) between the existent and being,[5] the "difference" or place between the two.

The ontologico-encyclopedic conclusion of the *Timaeus* seems to cover over the open chasm in the middle of the book. What it would thus cover over, closing the gaping mouth of the quasi-banned discourse on *khōra*, would perhaps not only be the abyss between the sensible and the intelligible, between being and nothingness, between being and the lesser being, nor even perhaps between being and the existent, nor yet between *logos* and *muthos*, but between all these couples and another which would not even be *their* other.

If there is indeed a chasm in the middle of the book, a sort of abyss "in" which there is an attempt to think or say this abyssal chasm which would be *khōra*, the opening of a place "in" which everything would, at the same time, come to take *place* and *be reflected* (for these are images which are inscribed there), is it insignificant that a *mise en abyme* regulates a certain order of composition of the discourse? And that it goes so far as to regulate even this mode of thinking or of saying which must be similar without being identical to the one which is practiced *on the edges* of the chasm? Is it insignificant that this *mise en abyme* affects the forms of a discourse on *places* [*places*], notably political places, a politics of place entirely commanded by the consideration of sites [*lieux*] (jobs in the society, region, territory, country), as sites assigned to types or forms of discourse?

II

Mise en abyme of the discourse on *khōra*, site [*lieu*] of politics, politics of sites [*lieux*], such would be, then, the structure of an overprinting without a base.

At the opening of the *Timaeus*, there are considerations of the guardians of the city, the cultivators and the artisans, the division of labor and education. Let us note in passing, although it is an analogy whose structure is formal and external: those who are raised as guardians of the city will not have anything that is properly their own (*idion*), neither gold nor silver. They "will receive the salary of their rank from those they protect" (18b). To have nothing that is one's own, not even the gold which is the only thing comparable to it (50a), isn't this also the situation of the site, the condition of *khōra*? This question can be asked, even if one does not wish to take it seriously; however formal it may be, the analogy is scarcely contestable. One can say the same thing about the remark which follows immediately (18c) and touches on the education of women, on marriage, and above all, with the most pronounced insistence, on the community of children. All possible measures must be taken in order to ensure that no-one can know and recognize as his own (*idia*) the children who are born (18c–d). In procreation (*paidopoiia*), any attribution or natural or legitimate property should find itself excluded by the very milieu of the city. If one bears in mind the fact that a moment ago the text had prescribed a similar education for men and for women, who must be prepared for the same activities and for the same functions, one can still follow the thread of a formal analogy, namely, that of the said "comparison" of *khōra* with the mother and, a supplementary sign of expropriation, with the nurse. This comparison does not assure it/her of any property, in the sense of the subjective genitive or in the sense of the objective genitive: neither the properties of a genetrix (she engenders nothing and, besides, possesses no property at all), nor the ownership of children, those images of their father who, by the way, is no more their owner than is the mother. This is enough to say about the impropriety of the said comparison. But we are perhaps already in a site [*lieu*] where the law of the proper no longer has any meaning. Let us consider even the political strategy of marriages. It manifests a relation of abyssal and analogous reflexivity with what will be said later about *khōra*, about the "riddles" or sieves (*seiomena*, 52e, 53a) shaken in order to sort or select the "grain" and the "seed"; the law of the better is crossed with a certain chance. Now from the first pages of the *Timaeus*, in a purely political discourse, are described the apparatuses intended to bring about *in secret* the arranging of marriages in order that the children will be born with the best possible naturalness. And this does not happen without some drawing of lots (*kléros*, 18d–e).

Let us explain it at once. These formal analogies or these *mises en abyme*, refined, subtle (too subtle, some will think), are not considered here, *in the first place* [*en premier lieu*], as artifices, boldness, or secrets of formal composition: the art of Plato the writer! This art interests us and ought to do so more still, but what is important in this very place [*ici même*], and first of all, independently of the supposed intentions of a composer, are the constraints which produce these analogies. Shall we say that they constitute a *programme*? A *logic* whose authority was imposed on Plato? Yes, up to a point only, and this limit appears in the abyss itself: the being-programme of the programme, its structure of pre-inscription and of typographic prescription forms the explicit theme of the discourse *en abyme* on *khōra*. The latter figures the place of inscription of *all that is marked on the world*. Likewise the being-logical of logic, its essential *logos*, whether it be true, probable, or mythic, forms the explicit theme of the *Timaeus*, as we shall yet have occasion to explain. Thus one cannot calmly, with no further ado, call by the name *programme* or *logic* the form which dictates to Plato the law of such a composition: programme and logic are apprehended in it, *as such*, though it be in a dream, and put *en abyme*.

Having taken this precaution with regard to analogies which might seem imprudent, let us recall the most general trait which both gathers and authorizes these displacements, from one place to the other "in" the "same" place [*lieu*]. It is obvious, too obvious even to be noticed, and its generality has, so to speak, no other limit than itself: it is precisely that of the *genos*, of the genus in all genders and genera, of sexual difference, of the generation of children, of the kinds of being and of that *triton genos* which *khōra* is (neither sensible nor intelligible, "like" a mother or a nurse, etc.). We have just alluded to all these genres of genres, but we have not yet spoken of the *genos* as race,[6] people, group, community, affinity of birth, nation, etc. Now we're there.

Still at the opening of the *Timaeus*, there is recalled an earlier conversation, a discourse (*logos*) of Socrates on the *politeia* and on its better government. Socrates sums it up, and these are the themes of which we have just spoken. In passing, he uses the word *khōra* (19a) to designate the place assigned to children: you must rear the "children of the good," transport the others in secret to another country, continue to keep them under observation, and carry out a further sifting operation in attributing to each his place (*khōran*). After this reminder, Socrates declares himself incapable of praising this city and its men. In this he feels himself to be comparable to the poets and imitators. And here is the *genos* or *ethnos*. Socrates claims to have nothing against the people or the race, the tribe of the poets (*poiētikon genos*). But allowing for the place and the conditions of birth as well as the education, the nation, or race of imitators (*mimētikon ethnos*) will have difficulty in imitating what it has remained alien to, namely, that which happens in actions and words (*ergois, logois*) rather than in spectacles or simulacra. There is also the genre or the tribe of the sophists (*tōn sophistōn genos*). Socrates privileges here again the *situation*, the relation to place: the genus of sophists is characterized by the absence of a proper place, an economy, a fixed domicile; these people have no domesticity, no house that is proper to them (*oikēsis idias*). They wander from place to place, from town to town, incapable of understanding these men who, being philosophers and politicians, *have (a) place* [ont lieu; from *avoir lieu*, or "to take place"—Ed.], that is, act by means of gesture and speech, in the city or at war. *Poiētikon genos, mimētikon ethnos, tōn sophistōn genos*, after this enumeration what remains? Well, then, you, to whom I am speaking now, you who are also a *genos* (19e), and who belong to the genre of those who *have (a) place*, who take place, by nature and by education. You are thus both philosophers and politicians.

Socrates' strategy itself operates from a sort of nonplace, and that is what makes it very disconcerting, not to say alarming. In starting by declaring that he is, a little *like* the poets, the imitators, and the sophists, incapable of describing the philosopher-politicians. Socrates pretends to rank himself among those who feign. He affects to belong to the *genos* of those whose *genos* consists in affecting: in simulating the belonging to a place and to a community, for example, to the *genos* of true citizens, philosophers, and politicians, to "yours." *Socrates thus pretends to belong to the genus of those who pretend to belong to the genus of those who have (a) place, a place and an economy that are their own.* But in saying this, Socrates denounces this *genos* to which he pretends to belong. He claims to speak the truth on the subject of it: in truth, these people have no place, they are wanderers. *Therefore I who resemble them, I have no place* [je n'ai pas de lieu]: in any case, as for me I am similar to them, I do not take place [*je n'ai pas lieu*], but if I am similar to them or if I resemble them, that does not mean that I am their fellow. But this truth, namely that they and I, if we seem to belong to the same *genos*, are without a place of our own, is enunciated by me, since it is a truth, from *your* place, you who are on the side of the true *logos*, of philosophy and politics. I address you from your place [*place*] in order to say to you that I have no place [*place*], since I am like those who make their trade out of resemblance—the poets, the imitators, and the sophists, the genus of those who have no place. You alone have place and can say both the place and the nonplace in truth, and that is why I am going to give you back the floor. In truth, give it to you or leave it to you. To give back, to leave, or to give the floor to the other amounts to saying: you have (a) place, have (a) place, come.

The duplicity of this self-exclusion, the simulacrum of this withdrawal, plays on the belonging to the proper place, as a political place and as a habitation. Only this belonging to place authorizes the truth of the *logos*, that is, also its political effectivity, its pragmatic and praxical [*praxique*] efficiency, which Socrates regularly associates with the *logos* in this context. It is the belonging of a *genos* to a proper place which guarantees the truth of its *logos* (effective relation of the discourse to the thing itself, to the matter, *pragma*) and of its action (*praxis, ergon*). The specialists of the nonplace and of the simulacrum (among whom Socrates for a moment affects to rank himself) do not even have to be excluded from the city, like *pharmakoi*; they exclude themselves by themselves, as does Socrates here in giving back the word. They exclude themselves by themselves, or pretend to do so, also, because they quite simply have no room [*pas de place*]. There is no room for them in the political place [*lieu*] where affairs are spoken of and dealt with, the *agora*.

Although the word was already uttered (19a), the question of *khōra* as a general place or total receptacle (*pandekhēs*) is, of course, not yet posed. But if it is not posed as such, it gestures and points already. The note is given. For on the one hand, the ordered polysemy of the word always includes the sense of political place or, more generally, of *invested* place, by opposition to abstract space. *Khōra* "means": place occupied by someone, country, inhabited place, marked place, rank, post, assigned position, territory, or region. And in fact, *khōra* will always already be occupied, invested, even as a general place, and even when it is distinguished from everything that takes place in it. Whence the difficulty—we shall come to it—of treating it as an empty or geometric space, or even, and this is what Heidegger will say of it, as that which "prepares" the Cartesian space, the *extensio* of the *res extensa*. But on the other hand, the discourse of Socrates, if not the Socratic discourse, the discourse of Socrates in this precise place and on this marked place, proceeds from or affects to proceed from errancy [*depuis l'errance*], from a mobile or nonmarked place, in any case from a space or exclusion which happens to be, into the bargain, neutralized. Why neutralized? If Socrates pretends to include himself among those whose *genus* is to have no place, he does not assimilate himself to them, he says he resembles them. Hence he holds himself in a third genus, in a way, neither that of the sophists, poets, and other imitators (*of whom he speaks*), nor that of the philosopher-politicians (*to whom he speaks*, proposing only to listen to them). His speech is neither his address nor what it addresses. His speech *occurs* in a third genus and in the neutral space or a place without place, a place where everything is marked but which would be "in itself" unmarked. Doesn't he already resemble what others, later, those very ones to whom he gives the word, will call *khōra*? A mere resemblance, no doubt. Only a discourse of the sophists' type would be so indecent as to misuse it. But to misuse a resemblance, isn't that to present it as an identity, isn't it to assimilate? One can also ponder the reasons for resemblance as such.

We are in the preamble, our preamble on the preamble of the *Timaeus*. There is no serious philosophy in introductions, only mythology, at most, said Hegel.

In these preambles, it is not yet a question of *khōra*, at least not of the one that gives place to the measure of the cosmos. However, in a singular mode, the very place of the preamble gives place, on the threshold, to a treatment of place, to an assigning of their place to interlocutors who will be brought to treat of it later. And this assignation of places obeys a criterion: that of the place of the *genos* with regard to the *proper place*. Now, one has never, it seems, taken into account, taken particular count of, such a staging [*mise en scène*]. It distributes the marked places and the unmarked places according to a schema analogous to the one which will later order the discourse on *khōra*. Socrates *effaces himself*, effaces in himself all the types, all the genera, both those of the men of image and simulacrum whom he pretends for a moment to resemble and that of the men of action and men of their word, philosophers and politicians to whom he addresses himself while effacing himself before them. But in thus effacing himself, he situates himself or institutes himself as a *receptive addressee*, let us say, as a *receptacle of all* that will henceforth be inscribed. He declares himself to be *ready and all set* for that, disposed to *receive* everything he's offered. The words *kosmos* and *endekhomenon* are not far away: "πάρειμί τε οὖν δὴ κεκοσμημένος ἐπ᾽ αὐτὰ καὶ πάντων ἑτοιμότατος ὢν δέχεσται"; "So here I am, all ready to accept it and full of drive for receiving everything that you will have to offer me" (20c). Once more the question returns: what does *receive* mean? What does *dekhomai* mean? With this question in the form of "what does X mean?" it is not so much a question of meditating on the *sense* of such and such an expression as of remarking the fold of an immense difficulty: the relationship, so ancient, so traditional, so determinant, between the question of sense and the sensible and that of receptivity in general. The Kantian moment has some privilege here, but even before the *intuitus derivativus* or pure sensibility has been determined as receptivity, the intuitive or perceptive relation to *intelligible sense* has always included, in finite being in general, an irreducible receptivity. It is true *a fortiori* for sensory intuition or perception. *Dekhomai*, which will determine the relation of *khōra* to everything which is not herself and which she receives (it/she is *pandekhēs*, 51a), plays on a whole gamut of senses and connotations: to receive or accept (a deposit, a salary, a present), to welcome, to gather, or even to expect, for example, the gift of hospitality, to be its addressee, as is here the case for Socrates, in a scene of gift and counter-gift. It is a matter of returning (*antapodidōmi*) the gift of the hospitality of (the) discourses. Socrates says he is ready to receive in exchange the discourses of which he becomes the welcoming, receptive, grateful addressee (20b–c). We are still in a system of gift and debt. When we get on to *khōra* as *pandekhēs*, beyond all anthropomorphy, we shall perhaps glimpse a beyond of the debt.

Socrates is not *khōra*, but he would look a lot like it/her if it/she were someone or something. In any case, he puts himself in its/her place, which is not just a place among others, but perhaps *place itself*, the irreplaceable place. Irreplaceable and unplaceable place from which he receives the word(s) of those before whom he effaces himself but who receive them from him, for it is he who makes them talk like this. And us, too, implacably.

Socrates does not occupy this undiscoverable place, but it is the one from which, in the *Timaeus* and elsewhere, *he answers to his name.* For as *khōra* he must always "be called in the same way." And as it is not certain that Socrates himself, this one here, is someone or something, the play of the proper names becomes more abyssal than ever: What is place? To what and to whom does it give place? What takes place under these names? Who are you, *Khōra*?

III

The permutations, substitutions, displacements don't only touch upon names. The staging unfolds according to an embedding of discourses of a narrative type, reported or not, of which the origin or the first enunciation appears to be always relayed, appearing to disappear even where it appears. Their mythic dimension is sometimes exposed as such, and the *mise en abyme*, the putting *en abyme* is there given to be reflected without limit. We no longer know whence comes at times the feeling of dizziness, on what edges, up against the inside face of what wall: chaos, chasm, *khōra*.

When they explicitly touch on myth, the propositions of the *Timaeus* all seem ordered by a *double motif*. In its very duplicity, it would constitute the philosopheme of the mytheme such as we just saw it being installed, from Plato to Hegel.

1. On the one hand, myth derives from play. Hence it will not be taken seriously. Thus Plato warns Aristotle, he gets in ahead of the serious objection of Aristotle and makes the same use of the opposition play/seriousness (*paidia/spoudé*), in the name of philosophical seriousness.

2. But on the other hand, in the order of becoming, when one cannot lay claim to a firm and stable *logos*, when one must make do with the probable, then myth is the done thing [*de rigueur*]; it is rigor.

These two motifs are necessarily interwoven, which gives the game its seriousness and the seriousness its play. It's not forbidden and not difficult to discourse (*dialogisasthai*, 59c) on the subject of bodies when one seeks only probability. One can then make do with the form (*idean*) of probable myths (*tōn eikotōn mythōn*). In these moments of recreation, one abandons reasonings on the subject of eternal beings; one seeks what is probable on the subject of becoming. One can then take a pleasure there (*hèdonèn*) without remorse; one can moderately and reasonably enjoy the game (*paidian*, 59d). The *Timaeus* multiplies propositions of this type. The mythic discourse plays with the probable image because the sensory world is itself (an) image. Sensory becoming is an image, a semblance; myth is an image of this image. The demiurge formed the cosmos *in the image* of the eternal paradigm which he contemplates. The *logos* which relates to these images, to these iconic beings, must be of the same nature: merely probable (29b–c–d). We are obliged to accept in this domain the "probable myth" (*ton eikota mython*) and not to seek any further (29d, see also 44d, 48d, 57d, 72d–e).

If the cosmo-ontologic encyclopedia of the *Timaeus* presents itself as a "probable myth," a tale ordered by the hierarchized opposition of the sensible and the intelligible, of the image in the course of becoming and of eternal being, how can one inscribe therein or situate therein the discourse on *khōra*? It is indeed inscribed there for a moment, but it also has a bearing on a *place of inscription*, of which it is clearly said that it *exceeds* or *precedes*, in an order that is, moreover, alogical and achronic, anachronistic too, the constitutive oppositions of mytho-logic as such, of mythic discourse and of the discourse *on* myth. On the one hand, by resembling an *oneiric* and *bastard* reasoning, this discourse reminds us of a sort of myth within the myth, of an open abyss in the general myth. But on the other hand, in giving to be thought that which belongs neither to sensory being nor to intelligible being, neither to becoming nor to eternity, the discourse on *khōra* is no longer a discourse on being, it is neither true nor probable and appears thus to be heterogeneous to myth, at least to mytho-logic, to this philosopho-mytheme which orders myth to its philosophical *telos*.

The abyss does not open all at once, at the moment when the general theme of *khōra* receives its name, right in the middle [*milieu*] of the book. It all seems to happen just *as if*—and the *as if* is important to us here—the fracture of this abyss were announced in a muted and subterranean way, preparing and propagating in advance its simulacra and *mises en abyme*: a series of mythic fictions embedded mutually in each other.

Let us consider first, in the staging of the *Timaeus*, from the outset, what Marx calls the "Egyptian model."[7] Certain motifs, which we could call *typomorphic*, anticipate there the sequence on the *ekmageion*, this print-bearer, that matter always ready to receive the imprint, or else on the imprint and the seal themselves, the imprinted relief (*ektupōma*)—these are so many tricks for approaching the enigma of *khōra*.

First occurrence: to write for the child. Such as it reaches us, borne

by a series of fictional relays which we shall analyze later, the speech
of the old Egyptian priest puts (something) forward in a way prior
to all writing. He opposes it to myth, quite simply. You Greeks, he
says to Solon, you are like children, for you have no written
tradition. After a cataclysm you have to reinvent everything. Here
in Egypt everything is written (*panta gegrammena*) since the most
ancient times (*ek palaiou*) (23a), and so too is even your own
history, the history of you Greeks. You don't know where your
present city comes from, for those who survive the frequent catas-
trophes die in their turn without having been capable of expressing
themselves in writing (23c). Deprived of written archives, you have
recourse in your genealogies to "childish myths" (23b). Since you
have no writing, you need myth.

This exchange is not without some formal paradoxes. As the
myth of its origin, the memory of a city is seen to be entrusted not
only to a writing but to the writing of the other, to the secretariat of
another city. It must thus *be made other* twice over in order to be
saved, and it is indeed a question of salvation, of *saving* a memory
(23a) by writing on the walls of temples. The living memory must
be exiled to the graphic vestiges of *another place*, which is also
another city and another political space. But the techno-graphic
superiority of the Egyptians is nonetheless subordinated to the
service of the Greek *logos*: you Greeks, "you surpassed all men in all
sorts of qualities, as befits the scions and the pupils of the gods.
Numerous and great were your exploits and those of your city: they
are here by writing [*gegrammena*] and are admired" (24d). The
memory of a people inspected, appropriated by another people, or
even by another culture: a phenomenon in the history of cultures
well known as the history of colonization. But the fact appears
highly significant here: the memory is deposited, entrusted to a
depot on the shores of a people which declares, here at least, its
admiration, its dependence, its subordination. The Egyptian is
supposed to have appropriated the culture of the Greek masters,
who now depend on this *hypomnesis*, on this secretariat's writing,
on these monuments: Thoth or Hermes, whichever you prefer. For
this discourse of the priest—or Egyptian interpreter—is uttered

here and interpreted in Greek, for the Greeks. Will we ever know who is holding this discourse *on* the dialectic of the master and the slave and on the two memories?

Second occurrence: to receive and perpetuate childhood. So Critias reports a tale of Solon, who himself reports the tale which an Egyptian priest told him on the subject of the *mythological* foundation, precisely, in the memory of the Athenians. Still more precisely: Critias repeats a tale which he had already told the night before and in the course of which he reported a conversation between Solon and Critias, his great-grandfather, a conversation which had been recounted to him when he was a child by his ancestor Critias, who himself had heard from Solon the account of the talk which the latter had had in Egypt with the old priest, the same one who explained to him, in short, why all the Greeks are at the mercy of oral tale-telling, of the oral tradition which, by depriving them of writing, destined them to perpetual childhood! So here is a tale-telling about oral tale-tellings, a chain of oral traditions by which those who are subject to it explain to themselves how someone else, coming from a country of writing, explains to them, orally, why they are doomed to orality. So many Greek children, then, ancestors, children and grandchildren, reflecting amongst themselves but thanks to the mediation of someone other, at once foreigner/stranger and accomplice, superior and inferior, the mythopoetics of oral tale-telling. But once again, this will not make us forget (since it is written!) that all this is written in that place which *receives* everything, in this case, namely, the *Timaeus*, and is therein addressed to the one who, as we do, and before us, *receives* everything, in this theory of receptions—Socrates.

At the end of these tales of tales, after these recountings that are mutually inscribed in each other to the point where one often wonders who is, after all, *holding* this discourse, who is *taking up* speech and who is *receiving* it, the young Critias recounts how he remembers all this. A tale about the possibility of the tale, a proposition about origin, memory, and writing. As I most often do, I quote a current translation (here that of Rivaud, in the Budé

edition [F. M. Cornford's translation, *Plato's Cosmology: The "Timaeus" of Plato* (Indianapolis: Bobbs-Merrill, n.d.) has been used,
and modified at need, in this English version—Tr.], modifying it or
mentioning the Greek word only where our context requires it:

> Accordingly, as Hermocrates has told you, no sooner had I left yester-
> day than I set about repeating the story to our friends as I recalled it,
> and when I got home I recovered pretty well the whole of it by
> thinking it over at night. How true it is, as they say [τὸ λεγόμενον] that
> what we learn in childhood [τὰ παίδων μαθήματα] has a wonderful
> hold on the memory [θαυμαστὸν ἔχει τι μνημεῖον]! I doubt if I could
> recall everything that I heard yesterday; but I should be surprised
> [θαυμάσαιμ'] if I have lost any detail of this story told me so long ago.
> I listened at the time with much childish delight, and the old man was
> very ready to answer the questions I kept on asking; so it has remained
> in me, as if painted with wax in indelible letters [ὥστε οἷον ἐγκαύματα
> ἀνεκπλύτου γραφῆς ἔμμονά μοι γέγονεν].   (26b–c)

In the space of so-called natural, spontaneous, living memory,
the originary would be better preserved. Childhood would be more
durably inscribed in this wax than the intervening times. Effacement would be the figure for the *middle* [*milieu*; Derrida plays on
this word with its suggestion of "half-way place," "something that
is only half place," *mi-lieu*—Tr.] both for space and for time. It
would affect only second or secondary impressions, average or
mediated. The originary impression would be ineffaceable, once it
has been engraved in the virgin wax.

Now what is *represented* by a virgin wax, a wax that is always
virgin, absolutely preceding any possible impression, always older,
because atemporal, than everything that seems to affect it in order
to take form *in it,* in it which *receives,* nevertheless, and in it which,
for the same reason, is always younger, infant even, achronic and
anachronistic, so indeterminate that it does not even justify the
name and the form of wax? Let us leave this question suspended
until the moment when there will be grounds for [*où il y aura lieu
de*] renaming *khōra.* But it was already necessary to show the
homology of this schema with the very content of the tales. In

truth, each narrative content—fabulous, fictive, legendary, or mythic, it doesn't matter for the moment—becomes in its turn the content of a different tale. Each tale is thus the *receptacle* of another. There is nothing but receptacles of narrative receptacles, or narrative receptacles of receptacles. Let us not forget that receptacle, place of reception or harboring/lodging (*hypodokhè*), is the most insistent determination (let us not say "essential," for reasons which must already be obvious) of *khōra*.

But if *khōra* is a receptacle, if it/she gives place to all the stories, ontologic or mythic, that can be recounted on the subject of what she receives and even of what she resembles but which in fact takes place in her, *khōra* herself, so to speak, does not become the object of any *tale*, whether true or fabled. A secret without secret remains forever impenetrable on the subject of it/her [*à son sujet*]. Though it is not a true *logos*, no more is the word on *khōra* a probable myth, either, a story that is reported and in which another story will take place in its turn.

Let us take it up again from farther back. In that fiction which is the *written* ensemble of the dialogue entitled *Timaeus*, someone speaks at first of a dialogue which is said to have taken place "last night" (*khthes*, 17a). This second fiction (F2) has a content, the fictive model of an ideal city (17c), which is described in a narrative mode. A structure of inclusion makes of the *included* fiction, in a sense the theme of the prior fiction, which is its *including* form, its capable container, let us say its receptacle. Socrates, who, as we have noted, figures as a general addressee, capable of understanding everything and therefore of receiving everything (like ourselves, even here), then affects to interrupt this mythopoetic string of events. But this is only in order to relaunch it even more forcefully:

I may now go on to tell you how I feel about the State [*politeia*] we have described. I feel rather like a man who has been looking at some beautiful creatures [*zōa kala*], either represented in painting [*hypo graphés*] or really alive but motionless, and conceives a desire to watch them in motion and actively exercising the powers promised by their form. That is just what I feel about the State we have described: I should like to hear an account of it putting forth its strength in such contests as a State will engage in against others, going to war in a manner worthy of, and achieving results befitting, the training and education given to its citizens, both in feats of arms and in negotiation with various other States.   (19b–c)

Desire of Socrates, of the one who receives everything, once again: to give life, to see life and movement given to a *graphé*, to see a zoography become animated, in other words, a pictural representation, the description or the dead inscription of the living. To give birth—but this is also war. And therefore death. This desire is also political. How would one animate this representation of the political? How would one set in motion, that is, set walking/marching, a dead representation of the *politeia*? By showing the city in relation to other cities. One will thus describe by words, by discursive painting, a State's movement of going outside of itself. Thanks to a *second graphic fiction*, one will go outside of the first *graphé*. The latter was more dead, less living than the second one to the extent that it described the city in itself, internal to itself, at peace with its own interiority, in its domestic economy. The possibility of war makes the graphic image—the description—of the ideal city go out, not yet into the living and mobile real, but into a better image, a living image of this living and mobile real, while yet showing a functioning that is internal to the test: war. In all the senses of the word, it is a *decisive exposition* of the city.[8]

At the moment when he asks that one should at last get out of this graphic hallucination to see the image of the things themselves in movement, Socrates points at, without denouncing them, poets and sophists: by definition they are incapable of getting out of the simulacrum or the mimetic hallucination in order to describe political reality. Paradoxically, it is to the extent that they are always outside, without a place of their own and with no fixed abode, that these members of the *mimetikon ethnos*, or the *genos tōn sophistōn* or of the *poiētikon genos* remain powerless, incapable of speaking of the political reality inasmuch as it is measured *on the outside*, precisely, in the test of war.

At the same time, affecting to rank himself on the side of this *ethnos* or of this *genos*, Socrates confesses that he too is incapable of going outside, by himself and of himself, of his mythomimetico-graphic dream in order to give life and movement to the city. ("I know myself well enough to know that I will never be capable of celebrating as one should this city and its citizens [in war, negotiation, and movement]. My incapacity is not surprising; but I have formed the same judgment about the poets," 19d.)

A supplementary irony: Socrates is not content to side for a moment with the men of the zoographic simulacrum; he declares that he does not despise their *genos* or their *ethnos*. This confers on the play between the text and the theme, between what is done and what is declared, as between the successive inclusions of the "receptacles" for themes and theses, a structure without an indivisible origin.

In this theatre of irony, where the scenes interlock in a series of receptacles without end and without bottom, how can one isolate a thesis or a theme that could be attributed calmly to the "philosophy-of-Plato," indeed to *philosophy* as the Platonic thing? This would be to misrecognize or violently deny the structure of the textual scene, to regard as resolved all the questions of topology in general, including that of the places of rhetoric, and to think one understood what it means to receive, that is, to understand. It's a little early. As always.

IV

Should one henceforth forbid oneself to speak of the philosophy of Plato, of the ontology of Plato, or even of Platonism? Not at all, and there would undoubtedly be no error of principle in so speaking, merely an inevitable *abstraction*. *Platonism* would mean, in these conditions, the thesis or the theme which one has extracted by artifice, misprision, and abstraction from the text, torn out of the written fiction of "Plato." Once this abstraction has been supercharged and deployed, it will be extended over all the folds of the text, of its ruses, overdeterminations, and reserves, which the abstraction will come to cover up and dissimulate. This will be called Platonism or the philosophy of Plato, which is neither arbitrary nor illegitimate, since a certain force of thetic abstraction at work in the heterogeneous text of Plato can recommend one to do so. It works and presents itself precisely under the name of philosophy. If it is not illegitimate and arbitrary to call it as it is called, that is because its arbitrary violence, its abstraction, consists in making the law, up to a point and for a while, in dominating, according to a mode which is precisely all of philosophy, other motifs of thought which are also at work in the text: for example, those which interest us here both by privilege and from another situation—let us say, for brevity, from another *historical* situation, even though history depends most often in its concept on this philosophical heritage. "Platonism" is thus certainly one of the effects of the text signed by Plato, for a long time, and for necessary reasons, the dominant effect, but this effect is always turned back against the text.

It must be possible to analyze this violent reversion. Not that we have at our disposal at a given moment a greater lucidity or new instruments. Prior to this technology or this methodology, a new situation, a new experience, a different *relation* must be possible. I leave these three words (*situation, experience, relation*) without complement in order not to determine them too quickly and in order to announce new questions through this reading of *khōra*. To say, for example, situation or topology of being, experience *of being* or relation *to being*, would perhaps be to set oneself up too quickly in the space opened up by the question of the meaning of being in its Heideggerian type. Now, it will appear later, a propos the Heideggerian interpretation of *khōra*, that our questions are also addressed to certain decisions of Heidegger and to their very horizon, to what forms the horizon of the question of the meaning of being and of its epochs.

The violent reversion of which we have just spoken is always interested and interesting. It is naturally at work in this ensemble without limit which we call here *the text*. In constructing itself, in being posed in its dominant form at a given moment (here that of the Platonic thesis, philosophy, or ontology), the text is neutralized in it, numbed, self-destructed, or dissimulated: unequally, partially, provisionally. The forces that are thus inhibited continue to maintain a certain disorder, some potential incoherence, and some heterogeneity in the organization of the theses. They introduce parasitism into it, and clandestinity, ventriloquism, and, above all, a general tone of denial, which one can learn to perceive by exercising one's ear or one's eye on it. "Platonism" is not only an example of this movement, the first "in" the whole history of philosophy. It commands it, it commands this *whole* history. A philosophy as such would henceforth always be "Platonic." Hence the necessity to continue to try to think what takes place in Plato, with Plato, what is shown there, what is hidden, so as to win there or to lose there.

Let us return to the *Timaeus.* At the point we have now reached, how can we recognize the *present* of the tale? Who is *presented* there? Who holds the discourse there? To whom is the speech addressed? Still to Socrates: we have already insisted on this singular dissymmetry: but that remains still too indeterminate, by definition. At this point, then, three instances of textual fiction are mutually included in one another, each as content given form in the receptacle of another: F1, the *Timaeus* itself, a unit(y) that is already difficult to cut up; F2, the conversation of the evening before (*The Republic, Politeia?* This debate is well known); and F3, its present résumé, the description of the ideal *politeia.*

But this is merely to begin (17a–19b). In front of the dead picture [*tableau mort,* a pun on *tableau vivant*—Tr.] Socrates thus demands that one pass on to life, to movement and to reality, in order to speak at last of philosophy and politics, those things that the *mimētikon ethnos,* the *poiētikon genos,* and the *tōn sophistōn genos* are, somewhat like Socrates, incapable of. He addresses his interlocutors as a different *genos,* and this apostrophe will make them speak while according to them the necessary right and competence for that. In effacing himself and in rendering up the word, Socrates seems also to induce and to program the discourse of his addressees, whose listener and receiver he affects to become. Who will speak henceforth through their mouths? Will it be they, Socrates' addressees? Or Socrates, their addressee? The *genos* of those who by nature and by education participate in the two orders, philosophy and politics ("ἅμα ἀμφοτέρων φύσει καὶ τροφῇ μετέχον," 20a), sees itself thus being assigned the word by the one who excludes himself from their *genos* and pretends to belong to the *genos* of the simulators.

So young Critias accepts (F4) to recount a tale which he had already told the night before, on the road, according to old oral traditions (*ek palaias akoès*, 20d). In the course of this tale, which, the night before, already repeated an old and ill-determined tradition, young Critias recounts another tale (F5), which old Critias, his ancestor, had himself told of a conversation which he (said he) had with Solon, a conversation in the course of which the latter relates (F6) in his turn a conversation which he (said he) had with an Egyptian priest and in the course of which the latter relates (F7) in his turn the origin of Athens: according to Egyptian scriptures.

Now it is in this last tale (the first one in the series of narrative events, the last one to be reported in this telling of tellings) that the reference to Egyptian writing returns. In the course of this first-last tale, the most mythic in its form, it is a matter of reminding the Greeks, who have remained children, of what the childhood of Athens was. Now, Athens is a figuration of a city which, though it did not have the correct usage of writing, nonetheless served as a model to the Egyptian city from which the priest came—hence as an exemplary paradigm in the place from which, in short, he advances this tale. That place, which seems to inspire or produce the tale thus has another place, Athens, as its model.

So it is Athens or its people who, as the apparent addressees or receptacles of the tale, would thus be, according to the priest himself, its utterers, producers, or inspirers, its informers.

In fiction F1—itself written, let us never forget that—there is thus developed a theory or a procession of writing referring, *in writing*, to an origin older than itself (F7).

In the center, between F3 and F4, is a sort of reversal, an apparent catastophe, and the appearance is that we think we're passing then at last into reality, exiting from the simulacrum. In truth, everything still remains confined in the space of the zoographic fiction. We can gauge the ironic ingenuity that Socrates needs in order to congratulate himself here on passing over to serious things and going beyond the inanimate painting to get on to real events at last. Indeed, he applauds when Critias announces to him that he is getting ready to recount what his grandfather told him Solon had told him on the subject of what an Egyptian priest had confided to him about "the marvelous exploits accomplished by this city" (20e), one of these exploits being "the greatest of all" (*pantōn de hen megiston*). Therefore, we will say (mimicking the argument of Saint Anselm, unless it be that of Gaunilon): an event which must have been *real*, or else it would not have been the greatest of all. That's well said, replies Socrates in his enthusiasm, *eu legeis*. And he goes on to ask at once what is this exploit, this *effective* work (*ergon*) which was not reported only as a fiction, a fable, something said, something one is content to talk about (*ou legomenon*) but also as a high fact really accomplished (*ontōs*) by that city, in former times about which Solon thus heard tell.

We ought, then, to speak at last of a fact (*ergon*) veritably, really accomplished. Now what happens? Let us note first that the essential would come to us from Solon's mouth, himself quoted by two generations of Critiases.

Now who is Solon? He is hastily presented as a poet of genius. If political urgency had left him the leisure to devote himself to his genius, he would have surpassed Hesiod or Homer (21a–b). After what Socrates has just said about poets, after the "realist" turn which the text pretended to take, this is a further excess of irony, which destabilizes even more the firmness of the theses and themes. It accentuates the dynamic tension between the thetic effect and the textual fiction, between on the one hand the "philosophy" or the "politics" which is here associated with him—contents of identifiable and transmissible meanings like the identity of a knowledge—and on the other hand a textual drift [*dérive*] which takes the form of a myth, in any event of a "saying" (*legomenon*), whose

origin appears always undefined, pulled back, entrusted to a responsibility that is forever adjourned, without a fixed and determinable subject. From one telling to the next, the author gets
farther and farther away. So the mythic saying resembles a discourse without a legitimate father. Orphan or bastard, it is distinguished from the philosophical *logos*, which, as is said in the
Phaedrus, must have a father to answer for it and about it. This
familial schema by which one situates a discourse will be found
again at work at the moment of situating, if we can still say this, the
place [*lieu*] of any site [*site*], namely *khōra*. On the one hand, *khōra*
would be the "receptacle—as it were, the nurse—of any birth"
("πάσης εἶναι γενέσεως ὑποδοχὴν αὐτὴν οἷον τιθήνην," 49a). As a
nurse, she thus drives from that *tertium quid* whose logic commands all that is attributed to it. On the other hand, a little further
on, another suitable "comparison" is proposed to us: "And it is
convenient to compare [*proseikasai prepei*] the receptacle to a
mother, the paradigm to a father, and the intermediary nature
between the two to a child [*ekgonon*]" (50d). And yet, to follow this
other figure, although it no longer has the place of the nurse but
that of the mother, *khōra* does not couple with the father, in other
words, with the paradigmatic model. She is a third gender/genus
(48e); she does not belong to an oppositional couple, for example,
to that which the intelligible paradigm forms with the sensible
becoming and which looks rather like a father/son couple. The
"mother" is supposedly apart. And since it's only a figure, a schema,
therefore one of these determinations which *khōra* receives, *khōra* is
not more of a mother than a nurse, is no more than a woman. This
triton genos is not a *genos*, first of all because it is a unique individual. She does not belong to the "race of women" (*genos gynaikōn*).[9]
Khōra marks a place apart, the spacing which keeps a dissymmetri-
cal relation to all that which, "in herself," beside or in addition to
herself, seems to make a couple with her. In the couple outside of
the couple, this strange mother who gives place without engendering can no longer be considered as an origin. She/it eludes all
anthropo-theological schemes, all history, all revelation, and all
truth. Preoriginary, *before* and outside of all generation, she no

longer even has the meaning of a past, of a present that is past. *Before* signifies no temporal anteriority. The relation of independence, the nonrelation, looks more like the relation of the interval or the spacing to what is lodged in it to be received in it.

And yet the discourse on *khōra*, conducted by a bastard reasoning without a legitimate father (*logismō tini nothō*; 52b), is inaugurated by a new return [*retour*] to the origin: a new raising of the stakes in the analytic regression. Backward steps [*retours en arrière*] give to the whole of the *Timaeus* its rhythm. Its proper time is articulated by movements which resume from even farther back the things already dealt with farther back. Thus:

> If, then, we are really [ὄντως] to tell how the world was born, we must bring in also the Errant Cause [καὶ τὸ τῆς πλανωμένης εἶδος αἰτίας] and in what manner its nature is to cause motion. So we must return upon our steps [πάλιν] thus, and take up again, for these phenomena, an appropriate new beginning [προσήκουσαν ἑτέραν ἀρχήν] and start once more upon our present theme from the beginning, as we did upon the theme of our earlier discourse [νῦν οὕτω περὶ τούτων πάλιν ἀρκτέον ἀπ' ἀρχῆς] (48a–b).

We will not begin again at the beginning. We will not go back, as is stated immediately after, to first principles or elements of all things (*stoikheia tou pantos*). We must go further onward, take up again everything that we were able to consider hitherto as the origin, go back behind and below [*en decà*] the elementary principles, that is, behind and below the opposition of the paradigm and its copy. And when, in order to do this, it is announced that recourse will be made only to probable affirmations ("τὴν τῶν εἰκότων λόγων δύναμιν," or again "τὸ τῶν εἰκότων δόγμα," 48d–e), it is in order also to propose to "divide further" the principle (48e): "Now let us divide this new beginning more amply than our first. We then distinguished two forms [δύο εἴδη] of being; now, we must point out a third [τρίτον ἄλλο γένος ἡμῖν δηλωτέον]."

Let us take things up again from farther back, which can be translated thus: let us go back behind and below the assured discourse of philosophy, which proceeds by oppositions of princi-

ple and counts on the origin as on a *normal couple*. We must go
back toward a preorigin which deprives us of this assurance and
requires at the same time an impure philosophical discourse,
threatened, bastard, hybrid. These traits are not negative. They do
not discredit a discourse which would simply be interior to philosophy, for if it is admittedly not true, merely probable, it still tells
what is necessary on the subject of necessity. The strange difficulty
of this whole text lies indeed in the distinction between these two
modalities: the true and the necessary. The bold stroke consists
here in going back behind and below the origin, or also the birth,
toward a *necessity* which is neither generative nor engendered and
which carries philosophy, "precedes" (prior to the time that passes
or the eternal time before history) and "receives" the effect, here the
image of oppositions (intelligible and sensible): philosophy. This
necessity (*khōra* is its sur-name) seems so virginal that it does not
even have the figure of a virgin any longer.

The discourse on *khōra* thus plays for philosophy a role analogous to the role which *khōra* "herself" plays for that which philosophy speaks of, namely, the cosmos formed or given form according
to the paradigm. Nevertheless, it is from this cosmos that the
proper—but necessarily inadequate—figures will be taken for describing *khōra*: receptacle, imprint-bearer, mother, or nurse. These
figures are not even true figures. Philosophy cannot speak directly,
whether in the mode of vigilance or of truth (true or probable),
about what these figures approach. The dream is between the two,
neither one nor the other. Philosophy cannot speak philosophically
of that which looks like its "mother," its "nurse," its "receptacle," or
its "imprint-bearer." As such, it speaks only of the father and the
son, as if the father engendered it all on his own.

Once again, a homology or analogy that is at least formal: in
order to think *khōra*, it is necessary to go back to a beginning that is
older than the beginning, namely, the birth of the cosmos, just as
the origin of the Athenians must be recalled to them from beyond
their own memory. In that which is formal about it, precisely, the
analogy is declared: a concern for architectural, textual (histologi-
cal) and even organic composition is presented as such a little

further on. It *recalls* the organicist motif of the *Phaedrus*: a well-composed *logos* must look like a living body. Timaeus: "Now that, like the builders [*tektosin*], we have the materials [*hylè*: material, wood, raw material, a word that Plato never used to qualify *khōra*, let that be said in passing to announce the problem posed by the Aristotelian interpretation of *khōra* as matter—JD] ready sorted to our hands, namely, the kinds of cause [necessary cause, divine cause—JD] we have distinguished, which are to be combined in the fabric [*synyphanthènai*] of reasoning [*logos*] which remains for us to do. Let us go back, then, once more, briefly, to the beginning [*palin ep'arkhēn*], and rapidly trace the steps that led us to the point from which we have now reached the same position once more; and then attempt to crown our story with a completion fitting all that has gone before [*teleutēn tōn mythō kephalèn*]" (69a).

TRANSLATED BY IAN MC LEOD

Notes

Notes

Passions

TRANSLATOR'S NOTE : I would like to thank Leslie Hill, Peter Larkin, and Will McNeill for their considerable help in uprooting errors and suggesting numerous felicitous phrasings and construals. Without their help this translation would have betrayed considerably greater linguistic eccentricity.

1. What does *the narrator* suggest on the subject of the analysis and the analyst in *The Purloined Letter*, but especially in the first pages of *The Murders in the Rue Morgue*? To give the greatest sharpness to the *un-rulebound* concept of the analyst, he suggests that the analyst would have to proceed beyond calculation, even without rules: "Yet to calculate is not in itself to analyze. . . . But it is in matters beyond the limits of mere rules that the skill of the analyst is evinced. He makes, *in silence* [my emphasis—JD], a host of observations and inferences. So, perhaps do his companions. . . . It will be found, in fact, that the ingenious are always fanciful, and the truly imaginative never otherwise than analytic." See Edgar Allan Poe, *Poetry and Tales* (New York: Library of America), pp. 388–89. In *The Purloined Letter* (ibid., pp. 691–92), Dupin quotes Chamfort and denounces as "folly" the *convention* by which mathematical reason would be "*the* reason *par excellence*," and as a perfectly *French* "scientific trickery" the application of the term "analysis" only to "algebraic operations." Note already, since this will be our theme, that these exchanges between the narrator and Dupin take place *in secret*, in a "secret place." Like them, with them, we are *au secret* [isolated, shut

away—Tr.], as we say in French, and "in the secret," which does not mean that we know anything. It is at least and precisely what the narrator, in a form written and published by Poe, *tells* (us): twice the secret is *told* (even the address supplied: "at an obscure library in the rue Montmartre," then "in a retired and desolate portion of the Faubourg St Germain," then "in his little back library, or book closet, No 33, Rue Dunôt, Faubourg St Germain" [ibid., p. 680]) without for all that the same secret ever being penetrated at all. And this is because it is all a matter of trace, both in the trace of discourse, and in the discourse of inscription, of transcription or, if one wishes to follow convention, of writing, both in the writing of literature, and in the literature of fiction, both in the fiction of narration, and placed in the mouth of a narrator, to whom, for all these reasons, nothing requires us to give credit. That a secret can be announced without being revealed, or, alternatively, that the secret is manifest, this is what there is [*il y a*] (*es gibt*) and will always remain to translate, even here, etc.

2. "I was deeply interested in the little family history which he detailed to me with all the candor which a Frenchman indulges whenever mere self is the theme" (Edgar Allan Poe, *The Murders in the Rue Morgue*, in *Poetry and Tales*, p. 400). "Je fus profondément intéressé par sa petite histoire de famille, qu'il me raconta minutieusement avec cette candeur et cet abandon—ce sans-façon du *moi*—qui est le propre de tout Français quand il parle de ses propres affaires" (Poe, *The Murders in the Rue Morgue*, trans. Charles Baudelaire in his *Oeuvres complètes: Histoires extraordinaires* [Paris: Louis Conard, 1932], p. 6). Is it enough to speak French, to have learned to speak French, to be or to have become a French citizen to appropriate for oneself, to appropriate oneself to, what is, according to Baudelaire's translation, so strictly personal—a translation more appropriating than appropriate—"le propre de tout Français" (the property of all French people)?

3. One ought not to have, *On devrait ne pas devoir*, even for reasons of economy, to dispense with here [*faire ici l'economie de*] a slow, indirect, uncertain analysis of that which, in *certain* determined linguistic and cultural regions [*aires*] (*certain*, hence not all nor all equally), would root duty in debt. Even before getting involved in that, we cannot detach ourselves from a feeling, one whose linguistic or cultural conditioning is difficult to assess. It is doubtless more than a feeling (in the most common sense of the term, that of the sensibility or the "pathological" of which Kant spoke), but we keenly *feel* this paradox: a gesture remains

a-moral (it falls short of giving affirmation, unlimited, incalculable, or uncalculating, without any possible reappropriation, against which one must measure the ethicity or the morality of ethics), if it was accomplished out of *duty* in the sense of "duty of restitution," out of a duty which would come down to the discharge of a debt, out of such a duty as having to return what has been lent or borrowed. Pure morality must exceed all calculation, conscious or unconscious, of restitution or reappropriation. This feeling *tells* us, perhaps without *dictating* anything, that we must go beyond duty, or at least beyond *duty as debt*: duty owes nothing, it must owe nothing, it ought at any rate to owe nothing [*le devoir ne doit rien, il doit ne rien devoir, il devrait en tous cas ne rien devoir*]. But is there a duty without debt? How are we to understand, how translate a *saying* which tells us that a duty ought to prescribe nothing [*un devoir doit ne rien devoir*] in order to be or to do what it should be or should do, namely, a duty, its duty? Here a discrete and silent break with culture and language announces itself, and it is, it would be, *this* duty.

But if debt, *the economy of debt*, continues to haunt all duty, then would we still say that duty insists on being carried beyond duty? And that between these two duties no common measure should resist the gentle but *intractable* [*intraitable*] imperative of the former? Now, who will ever show that this haunting memory of debt can or should ever cease to disturb the feeling of duty? Should not this disquiet predispose us indefinitely against the good conscience? Does it not dictate to us the first or the last duty? It is here that conscience and etymologico-semantic knowledge are indispensable, even if as such they must not have the last word. We must be content *here* with indicative references (*here* provides the rule: a place, a certain limited number of pages, a certain time, a *deadline* [English in original—Tr.], yes, time and space ruled by a mysterious ceremony). One would have to cross-reference between them, and try, if possible, to link them up in a network. One very accidental trajectory would follow the movements back and forth [*aller et retours*: also "return tickets"; "outgoing and returns" would perhaps capture a more financial idiom—Tr.), for example, between the determination of duty in *The Critique of Practical Reason* or *The Foundations of the Metaphysics of Morals*, the determination of debt and of culpability in the Kantian metaphysics of law, the meditation of *Being and Time* on the "attestation" (*Bezeugung*), call (*Ruf*), and on originary *Schuldigsein* (being-guilty), and (for example) the second essay of *The Genealogy of Morals* on "guilt" (*Schuld*), "bad conscience" (*Schlechtesgewissen*) and the like (*und Verwandtes*), in which Nietzsche begins (section 2) by recalling "the long history of the origin of *responsibility*" ("die lange Geschichte von der Herkunft der Verantwortlichkeit") and asks (section 4) whether "these genealogists of morality had ever had the faintest suspicion that, for example, the central moral concept of guilt [*zum Beispiel jener moralische Hauptbegriff "Schuld"*] draws its origin from the very material concept of 'debt' [*Schulden*]." In the same movement, Nietzsche recalls (section 6) the cruel aspect (*Grausamkeit*) of "old Kant's" categorical imperative. Freud would not be far away, the Freud of *Totem and Taboo* on the religions of the father and the religions of the son, on the origin of remorse and of the moral conscience, on the sacrifices and the puttings to death that they require, on the accession of the confraternal law (let us say, of a *certain concept* of democracy).

Accidental back and forth movements [*aller et retours*—see above, Tr.], comings and goings, then, between all these already canonical texts and meditations of a type apparently different but in fact very close—and closer to our time, for example, the most recent proposals of Emile Benveniste (*Indo-European Language and Society*, trans. Elizabeth Palmer [Miami: University of Miami Press, 1973], ch. 16, "Lending, Borrowing and Debt") or of Charles Malamoud (*Lien de vie, noeud mortel: Les Représentations de la dette en Chine, au Japon et dans le monde indien* [Paris: EHESS, 1988]). Two quotations will explain better, if more obliquely, the direction which I ought to pursue here, but cannot. One from Benveniste (pp. 148–49), the other from Malamoud (pp. 7, 8, 13, 14). Each quotation finds ample expansion, of course, in the work of these two authors.

Benveniste: "The sense of the Latin *debeo* 'owe' seems to result from the composition of the term *de + habeo*, a compound which is not open to doubt since the Latin archaic perfect is still *dehibui* (for instance, in Plautus). What does *debeo* mean? The current interpretation is 'to have something (which one keeps) from somebody': this is very simple, perhaps too much so, because a difficulty presents itself immediately: the construction with the dative is inexplicable, *debere aliquid alicui*.

"In Latin, contrary to what it might seem, *debere* does not constitute the proper expression for 'to owe' in the sense of 'to have a debt.' The technical and legal designation of the 'debt' is *aes alienum* in the expressions 'to have debts, to settle a debt, in prison for debt.' *Debere* in the sense of 'to have debts' is rare, it is only a derived usage.

"The sense of *debere* is different, although it is also translated by 'to owe.' One can 'owe' something without having borrowed it: for instance, one 'owes' rent for a house, although this does not involve the return of a sum borrowed. Because of its formation and construction, *debeo* should be interpreted according to the value which pertains to the prefix *de*, to wit: 'taken, withdrawn from'; hence 'to hold [*habere*] something which has been taken from [*de*] somebody.'

"This literal interpretation corresponds to an actual use: *debeo* is used in circumstances in which one has to give back something belonging to another and which one keeps without having literally 'borrowed' it: *debere* is to detain something taken from the belongings or rights of others. *Debere* is used, for instance, 'to owe the troops their pay' in speaking of a chief, or the provisioning of a town with corn. The obligation to give results from the fact that one holds what belongs to another. That is why *debeo* in the early period is not the proper term for *debt*.

"On the other hand, there is a close relation between 'debt,' 'loan,' and 'borrowing,' which is called *mutua pecunia: mutuam pecuniam solvere* 'pay a debt.' The adjective *mutuus* defines the relation which characterizes the loan. It has a clear formation and etymology. Although the verb *muto* has not taken on this technical sense, the connection with *mutuus* is certain. We may also cite *munus* and so link up with an extensive family of Indo-European words which, with various suffixes, denote the notion of 'reciprocity.' . . . The adjective *mutuus* indicates either 'loan' or 'borrowing,' according to the way in which the expression is qualified. It always has to do with money [*pecunia*] paid back exactly in the amount that was received."

Malamoud: "In the modern European languages to which we have just alluded, there appears to be a direct relationship between the forms of the verb *devoir*, which deal with obligation properly speaking or with obligation as probability, and those which mean 'being in debt [*dette*].' This relationship appears at one time in the fact that 'duty [*devoir*]' used absolutely is the equivalent of 'being indebted, being in debt,' with, when appropriate, a substantive complement indicating what debt consists of ('I owe [*dois*] a hundred francs'); at other times, in the very name of debt, which, in a more or less perceptible fashion for the speaker who is not an etymologist, derives from the verb *devoir* [should, ought, must—Tr.]: the debt, is what is *dû* [owed, due], what is carried into 'debit', the French term *dette* [debt], derives from the Latin *debitum*, which itself, past participle of *debere, devoir*, is used in the sense of 'debt.'

"In debt are combined duty and fault [*faute*; also lack]: a connection for which the history of the Germanic languages provides evidence: the German *Schuld* means both 'debt' and 'fault' [*faute*], and *schuldig* means both 'guilty' and 'debtor.' But *Schuld* derives from the Gothic *skuld*, which itself is connected with a verb *skulan* 'to have an obligation', 'to be in debt' (it translates, in the Gospel, the Greek verb *opheilō*, which has these two acceptations) and also 'to be at fault.' On the other hand, from the same Germanic radical, **skal*, but with another treatment of the initial letter, derives the German verb *sollen* 'should (do)' [*devoir (faire)*] and the English *shall*, which, although enjoying a specialist usage today in the expression of the future, meant, at a much older stage of the language, '*duty*' in the full sense.

"Groups of this type, more or less dense, more or less articulated, appear in a great number of Indo-European languages. They do not always delineate the same configurations, and each particular situation would demand a careful study. . . .

"The linguistic analyses of Jacqueline Pigeot for Japanese, of Viviane Alleton for Chinese, show, with all the requisite nuances, that the sphere of moral debt is clearly distinct from that of material debt, and that neither is connected with the morphemes corresponding to the word *devoir* [ought/should] as an auxiliary of obligation or of probability. The configurations that we notice in the languages that we have mentioned cannot be detected either in Japanese or Chinese. It is not quite the same for Sanskrit: there is no word *devoir* in Sanskrit, and there is no etymological connection between the different names for moral obligation and the name of debt. On the other hand, debt, named by a term which refers just as well to economic debt (including that which results from borrowing money with interest) as it does to moral debt, is presented, in Brahmanism, as the prototype and the principle by which debts are explained. . . .

"However, the notion of *créance* [belief, credence, credit, also debt, claim!—Tr.] can also lend itself to polysemic games: one only has to recall that in French *croyance* [belief] and *créance* are originally one and the same word, that in German *Gläubiger* means both *croyant* [believer] and *créancier* [creditor]. But the connection between *faire crédit* [to give credit] and *croire* [believe] is less fecund, ideologically, than that which binds *devoir* [duty/ought] to *être en dette* [being in debt]. . . .

"That man, according to Brahmanism, is born 'as debt', that this debt is the mark of his mortal condition, does not mean that human nature is

determined by original sin. As the Sanskrit word *rna, dette,* can sometimes be colored by *faute* [fault, lack], the German philologists of the last
century, influenced perhaps by the ambiguity of the word *Schuld,* as both
'debt' and 'fault', suggested making *rna* derive from the same Indo-
European radical as Latin: *reus,* 'accused', 'culpable.' The etymology is
erroneous, as would be a similarity between fundamental debt and
original sin. Debt is neither the sign nor the consequence of a fall, nor,
moreover, of any such occurrence. It does not result from a contract, but
directly places man in the condition or the status of debtor. This status
itself is made concrete and is diversified in a series of duties or of partial
debts, which are invoked, in the Hindu laws, to justify the rules of
positive law which organize the administration of material debt. . . .

"The most concrete example, and if we may say so, the best illustration
of this 'connection and drawing together [*colligence*] of heaven and earth'
which would be debt, was provided for us by Hou Ching-lang, who
shows us excellently how man buys his destiny by pouring into the
celestial treasury the bad money of a true sacrifice."

4. On this "problematic" of the semantic configuration of *cap,* of
capital, of the *capital,* of *front* (in the double sense of "front"—for
example, a military front or *faire front* [to face someone] as in *affronte-
ment* [face, brave, tackle], or *confrontation* [confrontation]—and the
prominence of the face, the *forehead* [English in original—Tr.]), of the
frontal and of the frontier, I would refer the reader particularly to my
L'Autre Cap, followed by *La Démocratie ajournée* (Paris: Minuit, 1991); in
English, *The Other Heading,* trans. Pascale-Anne Brault and Michael B.
Naas (Bloomington: Indiana University Press, 1992).

5. The child is the problem. As always. And the problem is always
childhood. Not that I am distinguishing here, as we used to do in my
student days, and in the tradition of Gabriel Marcel, between *problem*
and *mystery.* The mystery would rather depend here on a certain prob-
lematicity of the child. Later I will try perhaps to distinguish the *secret*
from both the *mystery* and the *problem.* In the Sophoclean tragedy which
bears his name, Philoctetus makes this supplementary use of the word
problema: the substitute, the deputy, the prosthesis, whatever or whoever
one *puts forward* to protect oneself while concealing oneself, whatever or
whoever comes in the place or in the name of the other, delegated or
diverted responsibility. It is at the moment when, abandoned by his
friends after a serpent bite had left a fetid wound on his body, Philoctetus
still keeps the secret of the Heraclean bow, an invincible bow from which

they will temporarily separate him. Right now, they are in need of both the weapon and the secret. Acting always indirectly, after many detours and stratagems, without ever facing him [*faire front*], Ulysses gives the order that the bow be seized. Philoctetus accuses, protests, or complains. He is astonished at the *offerings*, he no longer recognizes a child and bewails his hands: "Hands of mine [*O kheires*], quarry of Odysseus' hunting, now suffer your lack of the loved bowstring. You who have never had a healthy thought or noble, you Odysseus, how you have hunted me, how you have stolen upon me with this boy [Neoptolemus] as your shield [*labōn problema sautou paidia*]; because I did not know him that is no mate to you but worthy of me . . . now to my sorrow you have me bound hand and foot, intend to take me away, away from this shore on which you cast me once without friends or comrades or city, a dead man among the living. . . . To you all I have long been dead. God-hated wretch, how is it that now I am not lame and foul-smelling? How can you burn your sacrifice to God if I sail with you? Pour your libations? This was your excuse for casting me away" (1008–35; trans. David Grene in David Grene and Richmond Lattimore, eds., *The Complete Greek Tragedies, Sophocles II* [New York: Washington Square Press, 1967]).

6. I refer to the related treatment of the secret, the *stricture*, the Passion, and the Eucharist in *Glas* (Paris: Galilée, 1974), pp. 60–61; in in English, *Glas*, trans. John P. Leavey, Jr., and Richard Rand (Lincoln: University of Nebraska Press, 1986), pp. 50–51.

7. I have made use of the word *oblique* very often, too often and for a long time. I no longer remember where, nor in what context. In *Margins of Philosophy*, certainly (the *loxōs* of "Tympan"), and in *Glas*, in any case. Very recently, and in a very insistent way, in "Force of Law: The 'Mystical Foundation of Authority'" (in "Deconstruction and the Possibility of Justice," *Cardozo Law Review* 11, nos. 5–6 [1990]: 928, 934, 944–47; reprinted in Drucilla Cornell, Mark Rosenfeld, and David Gray Carlson, eds., *Deconstruction and the Possibility of Justice* [New York: Routledge, 1992], and in *Du droit à la Philosophie* [Paris: Galilée, 1990], esp. pp. 71ff). On the oblique inclination of *clinamen*, cf. "Mes chances: Au rendezvous de quelques stéréophonies épicuriennes," in *Confrontation* (Paris, 1988) (previously published in English in *Taking Chances* [Baltimore: Johns Hopkins University Press, 1984]).

8. Without asking his approval, I think I may quote certain fragments of the letter which he wrote to me on 28 May 1991. I leave it to the reader to decide how far this letter (including the entry for "oblique" from the

Oxford English Dictionary, which did not fail to accompany the consignment) will have prescribed the logic and the lexicon of this text. Perhaps I had already, again, uttered the word *oblique* in the course of an earlier conversation to which David Wood was thus referring. Fragments to share out, therefore, in the course of the ceremony, and David ventures to speak of "passion," as he ventures elsewhere to distinguish (perhaps to associate, *aut . . . aut* or *vel*, and without doubt to call up Shakespeare and the ghost of Marc Antony), praise and murder, praising to the skies and burying, "to praise" and "to bury." ("Its remit," he says of the book, "is neither to praise nor to bury Derrida, but . . ." but what, exactly?)

Here, then, is the fragment of the letter of 28 May 1991, and his "germ of a passion": "Dear Jacques, As you will see, I have taken you at your/my word, using my phrase 'an oblique offering' to describe what you agreed would be the only appropriate mode of entry into this volume. It is hardly suprising, perhaps, that the *most* oblique entry into this collection of already oblique offerings would be the most vertical and traditional auto-critique, or confession, or levelling with the reader (see e.g. S. Kierkegaard's 'A First and Last Declaration' at the end of *Concluding Unscientific Postscript*: 'Formally and for the sake of regularity I acknowledge herewith (what in fact hardly anyone can be interested in *knowing*) that I am the author, as people would call it of . . .' . . . This (and the whole sequence of thematizations of the interleavings of texts that you have offered us) suggests to me that the problem of an oblique entry might not simply be a problem, but a stimulus, the germ of a passion. Obviously, I would be equally happy (?) with something not yet published in English that would *function* in this text in an appropriate way: as a problematizing (or indeed reinscription) of the very idea of critique, as a displacement of the presumed subject of the collection ('Derrida'), as something that will *faire trembler* [French in the original, an allusion to Derrida's use of this expression in *De la grammatologie* (1967)—Tr.] the 'on' of writing *on* Derrida."

The allusive reference to Kierkegaard is very important to me here, because it names the great paradoxical thinker of the imitation of Jesus Christ (or of Socrates)—of the Passion, of attestation, and of the secret.

9. If elsewhere it has often forced itself upon me, the French word *intraitable* is doubtless difficult to translate. In a word, it can mean [*dire*] at one and the same time (1) what cannot be *traité* [treated, dealt with] (this is the impossible, or the inaccessible, it is also the theme of an impossible discourse: one would not know how to *thematize* it or to

formalize it, one would not know how to treat it [*en traiter*]); and (2) something whose imperative rigor or implacable law allows for no mercy and remains impassive before the required sacrifice (for example, the severity of duty or the categorical imperative). Which is as much as to say that the word *intraitable* is itself *intraitable* (for example, untranslatable) —and this is why I said that it had forced itself on me.

10. Other titles for this aporetic paradox: mimesis, mimicry, imitation. Morality, decision, responsibility, etc. require that one act without rules, and hence without example: that one never imitates. Mime, ritual, identifying conformity have no place in morality. And yet, the simple respect for the law, as (well as) for the other, this first duty, is it not to accept this iterability or this iterative identification which contaminates the pure singularity and untranslatability of the idiomatic secret? Is it by chance that, touching on this logic, Kant quotes, but *against the example*, the very example of *passion*, of a moment of the sacrificial passion of Christ, who provides the best example of what it is necessary not to do, namely, to offer oneself as an example. Because God alone—the best and only possible example?—remains, in Kant's eyes, invisibly secret and must himself put his exemplary value to the test of moral reason, that is, to a pure law whose concept conforms to no example. The reference to Mark 10: 17, and to Luke 18: 18, lies behind the passage in Kant's *Foundations of the Metaphysics of Morals*, which comes not long after the condemnation of suicide ("to preserve one's life is a duty"; "sein Leben Zu erhalten, ist Pflicht" [Berlin: de Gruyter]), 4: 397; trans. Lewis White Beck [New York: Bobs-Merrill, 1959], p. 14; hereafter, page numbers of the English translation will be in italic]; it is, in short, what one would like to reply to someone who invites you, directly or indirectly, to commit suicide or to sacrifice your own life): "Nor could one give poorer counsel to morality than to attempt to derive it from examples [*von Beispielen*]. For each example of morality which is exhibited to me must itself have been previously worthy to serve as an original example, i.e., as a model [*ob es auch würdig sei, zum ursprünglichen Beispiele, d.i. zum Muster, zu dienen*]. By no means could it authoritatively furnish [offer, *an die Hand zu geben*] the concept [*den Begriff*] of morality. Even the Holy One of the Gospel must be compared with our ideal of moral perfection before He is recognized as such: even He says of Himself, 'Why call ye me [whom you see] good? None is good [the archetype of the good, *das Urbild des Guten*] except God only [whom you do not see].' But whence do we have the concept of God as the highest good? Solely from the idea

of moral perfection which reason formulates a priori and which it inseparably connects with the concept of a free will. Imitation has no place in moral matters, and examples serve only for encouragement [*nur zur Aufmunterung*]. That is, they put beyond question the practicability of what the law commands, and they make visible that which the practical rule expresses more generally. But they can never justify our guiding ourselves by examples and our setting aside their true original [*ihr wahres Original*] which lies in reason" (4: 408–9; *25*). Elsewhere, in connection with the imperative of morality (*Imperatif der Sittlichkeit*): "But it must not be overlooked that it cannot be shown by any example [*durch kein Beispiel*] [i.e., it cannot be empirically shown] whether or not there is [*ob es gebe*] such an imperative" (4: 419; *37*). This is a most radical claim: no experience can assure us of the "there is" at this point. God himself cannot therefore serve as an example, and the concept of God as sovereign Good is an idea of reason. It remains that the discourse and the action (the passion) of Christ demonstrates *in an exemplary way*, singularly, par excellence, the inadequacy of the example, the secret of divine invisibility and the sovereignty of reason; and the encouragement, the stimulation, the exhortation, the instruction (*Aufmunterung*) is indispensable for all finite, that is to say, sensory beings, and for all intuitive singularity. The example is the only visibility of the invisible. There is no legislator that can be figured [*figurable*] outside reason. Put another way, there are only "figures" of the legislator, never any legislator *proprio sensu*, in particular any legislator to sacrifice (Moses, Christ, etc.). But no finite being will ever provide an economy of these figures, nor of mimesis in general, nor of anything that iterability contaminates. And passion is always a matter of example.

On the motives which act in secret (*insgeheim*), duty, sacrifice, example, and respect, it is necessary above all to return, of course, to the third chapter of Kant's *Critique of Practical Reason* ("The Motives of Pure Practical Reason").

11. *Apophasis*: [1657] "a kind of an Irony, whereby we deny that we say or do that which we especially say or do" (*Oxford English Dictionary*)— Tr.

12. *Geheimnis, geheim.* It is precisely in respect of duty that Kant often evokes the necessity of penetrating behind secret motives (*hinter die geheimen Triebfedern*), to see if there might not be a secret impulse of self-love (*kein geheimer Antrieb der Selbstliebe*) behind the greatest and most moral sacrifice (*Aufopferung*), the sacrifice that one believes can be

achieved properly by duty (*eigentlich aus Pflicht*), by pure duty (*aus reiner Pflicht*), when one accomplishes it in a manner solely in conformity to duty (*pflichtmässig*). This distinction is equivalent in Kant's eyes to that which opposes the letter (*Buchstabe*) to the spirit (*Geist*), or legality (*Legalität*) to moral legislation (*Gesetzmässigkeit*) (cf. further the beginning of ch. 3 of the *Critique of Practical Reason*). But if, as Kant then recognized, it is "absolutely impossible to establish by experience with complete certainty a single case" in the world in which one could eliminate the suspicion that there is a secret (that is to say, that which would allow us to distinguish between "out of duty" and "conforming to duty"), then the secret no more offers us the prospect of some interpretation [*déchiffrement*], even infinite, than it allows us to hope for a rigorous decontamination between "in conformity with duty" and "out of pure duty." Nor to finish with mimesis, whose principle of iterability will always connect the constitutive mimesis of one (the "in conformity with duty," *pflichtmässig*) to the nonmimesis constitutive of the other ("out of pure duty," *aus reiner Pflicht*), as nonduty to duty, nondebt to debt, nonresponsibility to responsibility, nonresponse to response. The decontamination is impossible not by virtue of some phenomenal or empirical limit, even if indelible, but precisely because this limit is not empirical; its possibility is linked *structurally* to the possibility of the "out of pure duty." Abolish the possibility of the simulacrum and of external repetition, and you abolish the possibility both of the law and of duty themselves, that is, of their recurrence. Impurity is principally inherent in the purity of duty, i.e., its iterability. Flouting all possible oppositions: *there* would be the secret [*là serait le secret*]. The secret of passion, the passion of the secret. To this secret that nothing could confine, as Kant would wish, within the order of "pathological" sensibility, no sacrifice will ever disclose its precise meaning. Because there is none.

13. In this paragraph I have translated *histoire* mostly as *story* (though *history* was usually also possible) except in those cases where *history* was clearly more appropriate—Tr.

14. I attempt elsewhere this "de-monstration" of the secret in connection with Baudelaire's *La Fausse Monnaie* (in *Donner le temps, 1: La Fausse Monnaie*, [Paris: Galilée, 1991]; *Given Time. 1. Counterfeit Money*, trans. Peggy Kamuf [Chicago: University of Chicago Press, 1992]). As for the *exemplary* secret of literature, allow me to add this note before concluding. Something of literature will have begun when it is not possible to decide whether, when I speak of something, I am indeed speaking of

something (of the thing itself, this one, for itself) or if I am giving an example, an example of something or an example of the fact that I can speak of something, of my way of speaking of something, of the possibility of speaking in general of something in general, or again of writing these words, etc. For example, suppose I say "I," that I write in the first person or that I write a text, as they say "autobiographically." No one will be able seriously to contradict me if I claim (or hint by ellipsis, without thematizing it) that I am not writing an "autobiographical" text but a text *on* autobiography of which this very text is an example. No one will seriously be able to contradict me if I say (or hint, etc.) that I am not writing about myself but on "I," on any I at all, or on the I in general, by giving an example: I am only an example, or I am exemplary. I am speaking of something ("I") to give an example of something (an "I") or of someone who speaks of something. And I give an example of an example. What I have just said about speaking on some subject does not require utterance [*la parole*], i.e., a discursive statement and its written transcription. It is already valid for every trace in general, whether it is preverbal, for example, for a mute deictic, the gesture or play of an animal. Because if there is a dissociation between myself [*moi*] and "I" [*"moi"*], between the reference to me and the reference to (an) "I" through the example of my "I," this dissociation, which could only *resemble* a difference between "use" and "mention" [both in English in original—Tr.], is still a pragmatic difference and not properly linguistic or discursive. It has not necessarily to be marked *in* words. The same words, the same grammar, can satisfy two functions. Simultaneously or successively. No more than in irony, and other similar things, does the difference between the two functions or the two values need to be thematized (sometimes it *must not*—and that is the secret), neither explained earnestly, nor even marked by quotation marks, visible or invisible, or other nonverbal indices. That is because literature can all the time play economically, elliptically, ironically, with these marks and nonmarks, and thus with the exemplarity of everything that it says and does, because reading it is at the same time an endless interpretation, a pleasure [*jouissance*] and an immeasurable frustration: it can always mean, teach, convey, more than it does, or at any rate something else. But I have said, literature is only exemplary of what happens everywhere, each time that there is some trace (or grace, i.e., each time that there is something rather than nothing, each time that *there is* (*es gibt*) and each time that it gives [*ça donne*] without return, without reason, freely, and *if there is* what there is then, i.e., *testimony, bearing witness*) and even before every *speech act* [English in original—Tr.] in the strict sense. The "strict" sense is, moreover, always extended by the structure of exemplarity. It is beginning from these undecidabilities or from these aporias, across them, that one has a chance of being able to accede to the rigorous possibility of *testimony,* if there is such a thing: to its problematic and to the experience of it.

I am always speaking about myself, without speaking about myself. This is why one cannot count the guests who speak or who squeeze around the table. Are they twelve or thirteen, or more or less? Each can be redoubled ad infinitum.

As this last note is a note on the first notes to which it could respond, let me add here: it is owing to this structure of exemplarity that each one can say: I can speak of myself without further ado [*sans façon*: also directly, without ceremony], the secret remains intact, my politeness unblemished, my reserve unbreached, my modesty more jealous than ever, I am responding without responding (to the invitation, to my name, to the word or the call [*appel*] which says "I"), you will never know whether I am speaking about myself, about this very self, or about another self, about any self or about the self in general, whether these statements concern [*relèvent de*] philosophy, literature, history, law, or any other identifiable institution. Not that these institutions can ever be assimilated (it has been said often enough, and who could contradict it?), but the distinctions to which they lend themselves become rigorous and reliable, statutory and stabilizable (through a long history, certainly) only so as to master, order, arrest this turbulence, to be able to make decisions, to *be able* tout court. It is of this, and for this, that literature (among other things) is "exemplary": it always is, says, does something other, something other than itself, an itself which moreover is only that, something other than itself. For example or par excellence: philosophy.

Sauf le nom

1. "Ben jenen Mystikern gibt es einige Stellen, die außerordentlich kühn sind, voll von schwierigen Metaphern und beinahe zur Gott-losigkeit hinneigend, so wie ich Gleiches bisweilen in den deutschen—im übrigen schönen—Gedichten eines gewissen Mannes bemerkt habe, der sich Johannes Angelus Silesius nennt" (Leibniz, letter to Paccius, 28 January 1695, in L. Dutens, ed., *Leibnitii opera* [Geneva, 1768]: 6:56).

Cited by Martin Heidegger, *Der Satz vom Grund* (Pfullingen: Neske, 1957), p. 68; *The Principle of Reason*, trans. Reginald Lilly (Bloomington: Indiana University Press, 1992), p. 35 [translation modified].

2. Aurelius Augustine, *Confessionum*, ed. Martin Skutella (Stuttgart: Teubner, 1981); *The Confessions of St. Augustine*, trans. Rex Warner (New York: New American Library, 1963), pp. 243, 212, 257, 210 (translation modified), 207, 212, 257 respectively—Trans.

3. Angelus Silesius (Johannes Scheffler), *Cherubinischer Wandersmann*, ed. Louise Gnädinger (Stuttgart: Philipp Reclam, 1984); *The Cherubinic Wanderer*, trans. Maria Shrady (New York: Paulist, 1986). The translation by Shrady, which is a selection, does not contain all the maxims cited and has been modified in the translations cited. Concerning the editions he uses, Derrida states: "*La Rose est sans pourquoi* [extracts from *Pélerin Chérubinique*, trans. Roger Munier (Paris: Arfuyen, 1988)]. I nearly always modify the translations and reconstitute the original transcription in Old German, as it is found published in the complete edition of *Cherubinischer Wandersmann*, by H. Plard [Paris: Aubier, 1946, bilingual ed.]. Some of the maxims cited refer to this edition and are not found in the extracts proposed by Roger Munier." In this English translation I have followed Gnädinger's critical edition and indicated the one significant difference of versions in brackets in maxim 4: 21—Trans.

4. Mark Taylor, "nO nOt nO," in Harold Coward and Toby Foshay, eds., *Derrida and Negative Theology* (Albany: State University of New York Press, 1992), pp. 176 and 186.

5. See, notably, J. Derrida, "Psyché: Invention de l'autre," in *Psyché: Inventions de l'autre* (Paris: Galilée, 1987), notably p. 59; "Psyche: Inventions of the Other," trans. Catherine Porter, in Lindsay Waters and Wlad Godzich, eds., *Reading de Man Reading* (Minneapolis: University of Minnesota Press, 1989), p. 60.

6. Numerous references to this subject are gathered in J. Derrida, *Donner le temps, 1. La Fausse Monnaie* (Paris: Galilée, 1991); *Given Time, 1. Counterfeit Money*, Peggy Kamuf (Chicago: University of Chicago Press, 1992).

7. Martin Heidegger, *Sein und Zeit*, 16th ed. (Tubingen: Niemeyer, 1986), §50, p. 250; *Being and Time*, trans. John Macquarrie and Edward Robinson (New York: Harper, 1962), p. 294. On this Heideggerian theme, cf. *Apories* (Paris: Galilée, 1994); *Aporias*, trans. Thomas Dutoit (Stanford: Stanford University Press, 1993).

8. "Comment ne pas parler," in *Psyché*.

9. For example, see ibid., pp. 168 and 187.

10. See J. Derrida, "The Politics of Friendship," trans. Gabriel Motz-kin, *The Journal of Philosophy* 85, 11 (November 1988): 632–44. That is the very schematic résumé of ongoing research on the history and the major or canonic traits of the concept of friendship.

11. Pp. 174 and 175.

12. Cf. "Nombre de oui," in *Psyché*; "A Number of Yes," trans. Brian Holmes, *Qui Parle* 2, no. 2 (1988): 120–33.

13. On Plotinus, see above, p. 70. On Heidegger and Lacan, cf. *Donner le temps*, pp. 12–13, n. 1.

Khōra

NOTE: The first version of this text appeared in *Poikilia: Etudes offertes à Jean-Pierre Vernant* (Paris: Ecole des Hautes Etudes en Sciences Sociales, 1987).

1. We hope to come back to this point, one of the most sensitive ones of our problematic, often and at length, in particular by sketching a history and a typology of the interpretations of *khōra*, or rather, when we shall try to describe the law of their paradoxes or of their aporias. Let us note for the moment only that in these two works—which, in the French language and separated by an interval of seventy years, propose a synoptic table and conclude with a general interpretation of all the past interpreta-tions—the meta-linguistic or meta-interpretative recourse to these values of metaphor, of comparison, or of image is never questioned for what it is. No question on interpretive rhetoric is posed, in particular, no ques-tion on what it necessarily borrows from a certain Platonic tradition (metaphor is a sensory detour for acceding to an intelligible meaning), which would render it little suited to provide a metalanguage for the interpretation of Plato and in particular of a text as strange as some passages of the *Timaeus* on *khōra*. Rivaud speaks thus of a "crowd of comparisons and metaphors whose variety is surprising" (p. 296), of "metaphors" and of "images" brought back to an "idea," that of the "in what" (p. 298), even if, against Zeller, he refuses to "see only metaphors in Plato's formulations" (p. 308). ("La Théorìe de la khōra et la cosmogonie du *Timée*," in *Le Problème du devenir et la notion de matière*, 1905, ch. 5).

Luc Brisson in turn speaks of "the metaphor of the dream used by Plato to illustrate his description" (*Le même et l'autre dans la structure ontologique au Timée de Platon*, 1974. p. 197, cf. also pp. 206, 207). He even systematizes operative recourse to the concept of metaphor and proposes classifying all the said metaphors at the moment of determining what he calls "the ontological nature of the "spatial milieu" (we shall come back later to this title and to the project it describes): "This [determining the "ontological nature" of the "spatial milieu"] poses a considerable problem, for Plato only speaks of the spatial milieu by using a totally metaphorical language, which gets away from any technical quality. That is why we shall first analyze two sequences of images: one of them bearing on sexual relations, and the other on artisanal activity" (p. 208, cf. also pp. 211, 212, 214, 217, 222).

Of course, it is not a question here of criticizing the use of the words *metaphor, comparison,* or *image.* It is often inevitable, and for reasons which we shall try to explain here. It will sometimes happen that we too will have recourse to them. But there is a point, it seems, where the relevance of this rhetorical code meets a limit and must be questioned as such, must become a theme and cease to be merely operative. It is precisely the point where the concepts of this rhetoric appear to be constructed on the basis of "Platonic" oppositions (intelligible/sensible, being as *eidos*/image, etc.), oppositions from which *khōra* precisely escapes. The apparent multiplicity of metaphors (or also of mythemes in general) signifies in these places not only that the proper meaning can only become intelligible via these detours, but that the opposition between the proper and the figurative, without losing all value, encounters here a limit.

2. Heidegger does this in particular in a brief passage, in fact a parenthesis, in his *Introduction to Metaphysics.* Let us do no more than quote here the translation, and we shall come back to it at length in the last part of this work: "(The reference to the passage in *Timaeus* [50d–e] is intended not only to clarify the link between the *paremphainon* and the *on,* between also-appearing [*des Miterscheinens*] and being as permanence, but at the same time to suggest that the transformation of the barely apprehended essence of place [*topos; Ortes*] and of *khōra* into a "space" [*Raum*] defined by extension [*Ausdehnung*] was prepared [*vorbereitet*] by the Platonic philosophy, i.e. in the interpretation of being as *idea.* Might *khōra* not mean: that which abstracts itself from every particular, that which withdraws, and in such a way precisely admits and 'makes place' [*Platz macht*] for something else?") (Pp. 50–51; English trans. by Ralph Manheim, Martin Heidegger, *An Introduction to Meta-*

physics [Garden City, N.Y.: Doubleday, 1961], p. 55, t.m.) Among all the questions posed for us by this text and its context, the most serious will no doubt bear upon all the decisions implied by this "is prepared" (*vorbereitet*).

3. *Vorlesungen über die Geschichte der Philosophie, Einleitung,* 8, 2b, *Verhältnis der Philosophie zur Religion, Werke* 18 (Frankfurt a. M.: Suhrkamp), p. 103.

4. Marcel Detienne and Jean-Pierre Vernant, *Les Ruses de l'intelligence, la métis des Grecs,* p. 66. Gaia is evoked by the Egyptian priest of the *Timaeus,* in a discourse to which we shall return. It is at the moment when he recognizes the greater antiquity of the city of Athens, which, however, has only a mythic memory and whose written archive is located as if on deposit in Egypt (23d–e). Cf. also Heidegger, *Nietzsche,* 1: 350: "Chaos, *khaos, khaine,* signifies the yawning [*das Gähnen*], the gaping, that which is split in two [*Auseinanderklaffende*]. We understand *khaos* in close connection with an original interpretation of the essence of the *aletheia* inasmuch as it is the abyss which opens (cf. Hesiod, *Theogony*). The representation of Chaos, in Nietzsche, has the function of preventing a 'humanization' [*Vermenschung*] of existence in its totality. The 'humanization' includes as much the moral explanation of the world on the basis of the resolution of a Creator, as its technical explanation on the basis of the activity of a great artisan [*Handwerker*] (the Demiurge)."

5. "An interpretation decisive [*massgebende Deutung*] for Western thought is that given by Plato. He says that between beings and Being there is [*bestehe*] the *khorismos*; the *khōra* is the locus, the site, the place [*Ort*]. Plato means to say: beings and Being are in different places. Particular beings and Being are differently placed [*sind verschieden geortet*]. Thus when Plato gives thought to the *Khorismas,* to the different location of beings and Being, he is asking for the totally different place [*nach dem ganz anderen Ort*] of Being, as against the place of beings." (*Was heisst Denken?* [Tübingen: Max Niemeyer, 1954], pp. 174–75, English translation by J. Glenn Gray, Martin Heidegger, *What Is Called Thinking?* [New York: Harper & Row, 1968], p. 227, t.m.) Later we shall return at length to this passage and its context.

6. This is one of the motifs which link this essay to the one I wrote on *Geschlecht* in Heidegger. Cf. the introduction to that essay, "*Geschlecht, différence sexuelle, différence ontologique,*" in *Psyché: Inventions de l'autre* (Paris: Galilée, 1987).

7. *Capital,* fourth section, 14, 5. In another context, that of a seminar

held at the Ecole Normale Supérieure in 1970 (Theory of Philosophical Discourse: The Conditions of Inscription of the Text of Political Philosophy—the Example of Materialism), these reflections on the *Timaeus* intersected with other questions which here remain in the background and to which I shall return elsewhere. Other texts were studied, in particular those of Marx and Hegel, for the question of their relation to the politics of Plato in general, or of the division of labor, or of myth, or of rhetoric, or of matter, etc.

8. The possibility of war breaks into the ideality, in the ideal description of the ideal city, in the very space of this fiction or of this representation. The vein of this problematic, which we cannot follow here, seems to be among the richest. It might lead us in particular toward an original form of fiction which is *On the Social Contract*. According to Rousseau, the state of war between States cannot give rise to any pure, that is purely civil, law like the one which must reign inside the State. Even if it has its original law, the law of the people (*genos*, race, people, ethnic group), war makes us come back to a sort of specific savagery. It brings the social contract out of itself. By this suspension, it also shows the limits of the social contract: it throws a certain light on the frontiers of the social contract itself and of the theoretical or fabulous discourse which describes it. Thus it is at the end of the book of this ideal fiction that Rousseau in a few lines gets on to the problems which he is not going to deal with. We would have to analyze closely this conclusion and these considerations on war, the singular relation which they maintain with *the inside* of the social contract at the moment where they open onto its outside. It is both a thematic relation and a formal relation, a problem of composition: Rousseau seems to rub his eyes so as to perceive the outside of the fable or of the ideal genesis. He opens his eyes, but he closes the book: "Chap. X, *Conclusion*. After having set down the true principles of political law and tried to found the State on this basis, it remains to support it by its external relations: which would include the law of nations, commerce, the law of war and conquest, public law, leagues, negotiations, treaties, etc. But all that forms a new object too vast for my short sight: I should have fixed it ever closer to me."

9. Cf. Nicole Loraux, "Sur la race des femmes," in *Les Enfants d'Athéna* (Paris: 1981, pp. 75ff). In the context which we are here delimiting, see also, in the preceding chapter. "L'Autochtonie: Une Topique athénienne," that which concerns Athens in particular: "nurse (*trophos*), fatherland, and mother at the same time" (*Panegyric* of Isocrates) and the

"rival and complementary poles, *logos* and *mythos*" which "share the theatrical stage, in mutual confrontation but also in complicity" (pp. 67–72). As for the race of men (*genos anthropōn*), the Egyptian priest of the *Timaeus* assigns "places" to it: these are the places propitious for memory, for the conservation of archives, for writing and for tradition, these temperate *zones* which provide protection from destruction by excesses of heat and cold (22e–23a).

M E R I D I A N

Crossing Aesthetics

Library of Congress
Cataloging-in-Publication Data

Derrida, Jacques.
[Selections. English. 1995]
On the name / Jacques Derrida ;
edited by Thomas Dutoit.
    p.   cm. — (Meridian)
Includes bibliographical references.
Contents: Translating the name? /
by Thomas Dutoit — Passions —
Sauf le nom (Post-scriptum) — Khōra
ISBN 0-8047-2554-3 :   — ISBN 0-8047-2555-1 (pbk.) :
1. Emotions (Philosophy)   2. Names.   3. Plato.
Timaeus.   4. Deconstruction.   I. Dutoit, Thomas.
II. Derrida, Jacques. Passions. English.   III. Derrida, Jacques.
Sauf le nom.   English.   IV. Derrida, Jacques. Khōra.
English.   V. Title.   VI. Series: Meridian (Stanford, Calif.)
B2430.D482E5   1995
194—dc20
94-42209
CIP

⊗ This book is printed on acid-free paper.
It was typeset in Adobe Garamond and Lithos
by Keystone Typesetting, Inc.